Practicing Law: Solo & Small Firm

Nick Bauer

Practicing Law: Solo & Small Firm

ISBN: 978-1-883114-02-2

Print Edition 2020
Manufactured in the United States of America

Cover Photo by Nick Bauer
Monroe County Courthouse, Bloomington, Indiana

Cover Design and Book Layout by
Mesoscale Media, LLC

Mesoscale Media LLC
Bloomington, Indiana

Published by
Barnes & Bauer Enterprises

B&B
Bloomington, Ind.

Table of Contents

Acknowledgements

This book would not be the great resource it is today without the attorneys and judges who spoke to me and answered questions to offer a real-world perspective on solo and small practice. The knowledge and experience of these individuals are included throughout the book as well as full text of the interviews in Appendix A. Thank you to Matt Lloyd, Catherine Stafford, Vince Taylor, Steven Douglas, Jawn Bauer, and a background source who wished to remain anonymous. The legal community, at least in my hometown of Bloomington, Indiana, is certainly willing to help law students and young lawyers.

I also owe a great deal of thanks to Shana, my supervising professor for this project, a great teacher, and a fantastic friend.

The Career Services Office at the Maurer School of Law offered great support on this project as well with resources, connections for interviews, and encouragement. Specifically, thank you to Dean McFadden and Kim Bunge.

A wide variety of canines spent time with me during law school and during the writing of this book. Thanks to Asher, Max, and Ellie for reminding me to go play outside.

Finally, thank you to my parents, Jawn and Karen, who raised me in a small law firm and have made my life in Bloomington wonderful since day one. And they are willing to take on a new, young associate at the law firm.

About This Book

This book is not intended to be either comprehensive or authoritative by any stretch of the imagination. The idea is to highlight areas of running a solo or small law firm that a young attorney needs to think about that they would not have to think about in a large firm or government position. The goal is to offer topics of thought and enough information to see the responsibility and the flexibility that comes with being the boss at a solo or small firm.

Law schools do not teach students how to run a law firm or even to a certain extent how to practice law. Certainly, that will vary from school to school and is evolving as more clinical opportunities grow within the academic setting. Attorneys who have been in practice since the 1970s and 1980s said they had to learn to practice law because they were not taught that in school. Even graduates in the class of 2020 have a lot of gaps to fill in from on the job experience. For the solo or small firm attorney, this goes beyond practicing law and encompasses running a business. Law schools are even less prepared to teach law students about accounting and finance and running a successful business.

Hopefully this book inspires future law students to consider solo and small practice, but to go into it with their eyes opened to the many facets of practicing law while running a business. The task is possible, but without proper expectations and planning could be quite overwhelming.

Introduction

Many law students do not hear too much about solo and small practice while in law school. The focus tends to gravitate towards the big law firms who offer large starting salaries. According to 2017 U.S. Census data, 89.6% of law firms in the nation have fewer than ten lawyers and represent more than one third of all lawyers in private practice. Small firms are not necessarily overlooked, but career services offices may not hear from these offices as much because they do not hire with the regularity of the biggest firms.

The goal for this book is to find the novelties of setting up a solo or small firm as compared to going into a big firm or government office. The book highlights the added economic responsibilities on the new lawyer and any relevant ethical considerations or rules that will inform those decisions.

A solo or small firm practice can provide great benefits to a law student entering private practice after graduation unheard of in a big firm – flexible work hours, control over the cases you take, and no outlandish billable hours requirements. At the same time, lawyers in small firms are responsible for meeting payroll for the staff, maintaining an office space, and worrying about finding clients.

Solo or small practice is not for everyone. This book will be a success if it helps some law students see the pros and cons of choosing a smaller firm or hanging out their shingle. Solo and small practice is a worthwhile and respectable pursuit with great benefits for the attorney and the community where they practice. But, it is not for everyone.

I ended up writing this book out of necessity to graduate but also out of a strong interest in the topic personally. In my final semester of my third year of law school at the Indiana University Maurer School of Law, I learned on the first day of classes that the school canceled a class I signed up for – credit hours I needed to graduate. I scrambled to find an alternative and decided to do a directed research project.

One of my best professors, Professor Shana Wallace, agreed to take on yet another obligation in her busy life to supervise my project. I then needed a topic. Shana teaches, among other classes, the Legal Professions course at Maurer and I am going into practice at a small law firm after I graduate. As it turns out, the topic of solo and small firm practice was a way for me to learn about my future in practice and build a resource to leave in the Career Services Office for future students. I was also able to network with members of the local bar that I will join upon becoming a licensed attorney.

My father is an attorney in Bloomington, Indiana, my hometown and where my law school is located. I will be working for him as an associate attorney at his firm after passing the Indiana bar exam. The firm has two attorneys. I will be the third attorney in the office. I spent my childhood following a small firm attorney around. The fact that my father is a small firm, county seat lawyer influenced my decision.

I knew I did not want to go into a large law firm after working at a large accounting firm. I worked as an accountant for six years before enrolling in law school. I had first-hand experience with an environment that prioritized the billable hour over a personal life, such as coworkers acting like taking a lunch break to get away from your desk was an act of revolt. In comparison, I knew that my father worked very hard and took a lot of phone calls after hours, but he had control of his practice and his schedule. I have long had an inclination to work for myself or in a small business, and now I am very close to entering a small practice. I cannot wait.

/ngb
May 23, 2020

Chapter 1: Choosing Solo or Small Practice

Chapter Highlights

Why Solo or Small Practice is Different

- **Billable Hours** – Lower requirements compared to large law firms can lead to a better quality of life.

- **Compensation** – Starting salaries at large firms are higher than small firms, but solo and small firm attorneys can earn comfortable incomes.

- **Freedom and Flexibility** – Small firms offer far greater flexibility in choosing your clients, choosing your colleagues, and creating a schedule that balances work and life.

Consider if Solo and Small Practice is Right For You

- Solo and small practice provides more client contact early in your career as well as prestige in the community if your name is on the sign.

- You are an entrepreneur with responsibility for finding clients and running the business.

- A young lawyer in a solo or small practice has to be prepared to learn everything largely on their own.

Why Solo or Small Practice is Different

The same competence, due diligence, conflicts checks, and ethical standards apply to any lawyer, no matter the firm size or if in a government position. But, there are heightened responsibilities for a young lawyer in a solo or small firm not present for a young lawyer in a big firm or government job.

The solo or small firm attorney is an integral part of the day to day operations of the firm, if not a business owner. A recent law school graduate going into solo or small practice needs to find office space, manage firm finances, pay rent and utilities and payroll, handle fee collections, find clients, and so much more. Solo and small firm attorneys are not simply employees clocking in and clocking out and taking assigned work from partners.

Billable Hours

The simple fact is that billable hours requirements at the bigger law firms leave little time outside of work for an associate to enjoy life. A paper from the Yale Law School Career Development Office illustrated the math nicely.[1] At the low end of minimum billable hour requirements of 1800 hours per year, an associate will be at work a minimum of ten hours per day. The calculations assume the associate takes three weeks of vacation, two weeks for holidays, and no sick days or personal days.

In larger firms with higher billable hour requirements, the associate will need to work twelve hours per day each week plus seven hours on three Saturdays per month. This calculation is for a 2200 billable hour requirement and also allows for three weeks of vacation, two weeks for holidays, and no sick days or personal days.

But wait, there's more! The calculations referenced above are for actual time in the office working at a 70 to 75-percent efficiency or conversion rate (the amount of an hour spent at work that is billable to a client). In the legal profession, an efficiency of 75-80 percent of time billed is considered high.[2] New attorneys are typically less efficient. The associate at the large firm does not live in the office, even if it might feel that way most weeks. Adding in commute time lengthens the day by fifteen or thirty minutes, even an hour in a big city, on either side of the ten or twelve hours at work. Each day at work can bring the unexpected. Personal phone calls, interviewing candidates for new positions, mentoring interns, attending a doctor's appointment, pro bono work, and so many other activities can decrease your conversion rate of each hour in the day into a billable hour.

Over half of all firms with more than 250 attorneys require at least 1,900 billable hours per associate per year according to the National Association of Law Placement.[3] One commentator refers to these high billable hours requirements as "that feeling of Sisyphus endlessly pushing a rock up a hill."[4] The environment encourages a reluctance to take vacations, regularly working on weekends and holidays, and mental health problems. An old saying refers to working in a big law firm as "a pie-eating contest where the winner gets more pie."[5]

A majority of firms under 100 attorneys require fewer than 1,900 billable hours per year. The numbers are not broken down further by smaller size increments for firms under 100 attorneys, but the smaller firms of 1 to 10 lawyers have much lower requirements, if any. Anecdotally, an attorney in a firm of three lawyers and an attorney in a firm of four lawyers both bill around 800 hours per year.[6] Applying the logic of the Yale calculations, these attorneys bill about 3.4 hours per day working 47 weeks out of the year. Solo and small practice attorneys in smaller towns spend time running the business, talking to potential clients, and going to and from court, mediations, and other meetings outside of their office weekly and even daily.

⚖️ *Quotes from the Bar*

"I thought that I would have a better quality of life practicing in a smaller community and being the master of my fate, rather than being part of a larger organization."

– Background Source

"When you're talking about firm life, the big thing that you need to understand is they own you. And I use those words very deliberately. I don't know a big firm where if you're a new associate and you're not billing out at 60 hours a week, you're not going to be there two years. And just because you put in 60 hours doesn't mean that you're going to be billing 60 hours. So you're talking 90 hours minimum to bill out 60 hours. You really don't have that much of a life."

– Steven Douglas

"I never envisioned myself working for someone else. The primary benefit for me as a solo attorney was to be my own boss. There were additional benefits that flowed from that including scheduling your own time, allowing extra time to raise your family by being able to attend all school activities and sports and events for your children, travel, and enjoying leisure time."

– Jawn Bauer

Compensation

Law school graduates are seeking something in return for the long hours they will work at the bigger law firms. For most graduates, that is the high starting salaries. In general, firms of fewer than 100 attorneys average under $100,000 in starting salary, while firms with more than 100 attorneys average more than $100,000 in starting pay. Almost 70% of graduates entering firms with 1-10 lawyers earn more than $50,000 per year on average. (For more details on salaries and other statistics, see Appendix B)

A 2018 report from the National Center for Education Statistics found 69 percent of law school graduates had student loan debt at graduation. The average total student loan debt for law school graduates totaled $145,500.[7] Higher income will help pay down debt faster, simply put. Additionally, in solo and small firms less than half of all attorneys have paid time off work, dental and vision insurance, and a retirement plan with an employer matching contribution. Starting off, a new law school graduate may simply like the certainty of a paycheck and benefits.

In the long term, solo and small practice can provide a great living for an attorney. In a 2018 survey of almost 7,000 full time attorneys in solo and small law firms the average income was $194,000 with a median income of $135,000.[8] Some areas of practice, such as medical malpractice and personal injury, average more than $250,000 in yearly earnings. When you factor in that solo and small firms tend to be in smaller towns versus big cities, the money can go further in terms of cost of living.

A graduate in a small practice earning $60,000 and billing 800 hours a year makes $75 per hour. A graduate at a large firm earning $120,000 and billing 2,000 hours a year makes $60 per hour. These are simplified numbers with many variables, but the actual bottom line compensation for your time in a small firm is not drastically different than a large firm.

As a solo practitioner, if you land a big client or win a big case with a contingency fee arrangement, the entire benefit goes to you, not to the partners in charge of the firm where you are merely an employee.[9] In addition to the income, you personally gain the recognition and the boost in your reputation for a job well done.[10] The clients you served successfully will bring their future legal needs to you and send new clients by way of referrals. This future work is yours, not the big firm's despite you doing the hard work.[11]

Freedom and Flexibility

Not all benefits derived from a job come in the form of cash compensation. A small firm offers a great deal of freedom for attorneys. As Steven Douglas said, "The connection to the client is what is different in a small firm in my experience, it is much more personal than it is with a big firm." This was also a point made by Catherine Stafford, who appreciated "the chance to really decide for myself what areas of law I wanted to practice and who I wanted as clients." Larger firms do not give the same degree of freedom to choose work in this way.

The added responsibilities of being in a small firm open added benefits that most young associates will not find elsewhere. As one attorney put it, "I can tell you exactly the term that drove me to small practice instead of a big firm: the term is quality of life." Attorney Matt Lloyd echoed this sentiment when he talked about the benefits of a small firm, saying, "Flexibility, it cannot be beat. As the owner, it seems like I'm always on email whether I'm here in the office or not, but my flexibility is something I just cannot put a value on." Other attorneys spoke fondly of the opportunity to never miss a ball game for their kids, to attend school functions, and help members of their community.

⚖️ *Quotes from the Bar*

"I think the biggest part of small practice for me was the opportunity to pick my colleagues."

    – Catherine Stafford

"I have that option of saying, you know, this really isn't something I deal with and so, here are a couple names of some local practitioners who can help you. That's a tremendous freedom."

    – Steven Douglas

Consider if Solo and Small Practice is Right For You

Some reasons to start your own firm or work in a smaller firm where you play a more integral part include personality, client contact, practical training, money, type of legal work, security, and fringe benefits.[12] Certain individuals are more at home as an entrepreneur running a business than as a small piece of a larger corporation or entity. Some young attorneys may want to interact with clients while others prefer to work in the background. Being part of a small firm, particularly one you start and have your name on the sign out front, brings a level of prestige in a small town that is desirable for many practicing lawyers. There are lawyers who start a firm because they want to and lawyers who start a firm because they must.[13] If there are not jobs available due to a down economy, global pandemic, or other reasons, the best choice might be to hang your own shingle. A law license carries with it the ability to practice law and earn an income.

As Vince Taylor put it, "If you really want to find a job, you do one of two things: you either decide you want to practice a particular type of law and you're willing to go anywhere to do it, or you decide where you want to be, and if you go there, you're willing to do any kind of law you need to do to survive there." This is like the saying, "Go where the clients are."[14] If you do not have connections somewhere, you should go where clients need you. "If you are from a community where you have a lot of friends and family, then this is where you should locate."[15]

Even if you have a community with good connections, it takes time to build a practice. As Steven Douglas put it,

> "The first thing a recent graduate opening a law firm needs to understand is that there's not going to be a line of people. If you decide to throw out a shingle, to expect a line of people waiting at your door, the first day that you open your office, begging for your legal services, that doesn't happen. You're going to have to establish a practice. The old saying used to be, 'If you take care of a law practice for 10 years, it will take care of you for the rest of your life.'"

You have to establish yourself. As Vince Taylor said, "The hardest thing when starting a solo practice is that you have to be prepared to learn everything on your own. You don't have people teaching you things." You will be learning how to practice law as well as how to interact with clients and build your practice and reputation in the community.

> ### 🔨 *Rules of Professional Conduct*
>
> "The practice of law is a profession, not merely a business. Clients are not commodities that can be purchased and sold at will."
>
> **Model Rules of Professional Conduct, Rule 1.17, Comment 1**

Big firms have billable hours requirements for business and budgetary purposes. The firms need an associate to bill enough hours to pay for their high salary and benefits, pay for the cost of running a firm, and to generate a profit. Different attorneys view the practice of law differently, as you might expect. Back of the napkin notes look like the older generation of attorneys tend to view practicing law more as a profession than a business, with new attorneys thinking about the business side as being more important.

One attorney said of small practice, "The difficult part in a small firm is that you have to do both. You have to be the business side, you have to make sure you're making enough money to live on and to meet your obligations and your goals and so forth, while serving your clients." This attorney has been licensed to practice law for almost fifty years. They put being an attorney in perspective by saying, "The way I look at the practice of law, historically, there were three professions: medicine, law, and the clergy. Those are the three professions. In recent times, anybody engaged in a business has hijacked the term profession." Attorneys have a higher standard to live up to in their careers is the message.

In contrast, a younger attorney, Steven Douglas, says, "The best advice which I did not follow immediately was from my accountant, my CPA, who said, 'You are no longer an attorney. You are a businessman that sells legal services.'" That is not to say that a business-minded attorney does not respect the profession or that an attorney who thinks of themselves as a professional does not earn a proper living. There is a subtle yet noticeable difference in perspective, though.

A solo or small firm attorney needs to be mindful of both the business side and the profession of practicing law. The lawyer who fails to run the business will struggle financially to stay in business, while the attorney who does not serve the clients responsibly will run afoul of ethics rules or develop a poor reputation around town. If you own and run a small law firm, you have to take both aspects of the practice seriously to be successful.

If you own a firm, you must be prepared to run a business. One commentator says to ask yourself three questions in this regard: "(1) Do I actually want to be involved in the entire running of the business? (2) Am I committed to being a business owner and leader – not just an attorney? (3) Do I consider the time I spend working on the business as important as my billable work?"[16] You cannot let either side lag behind or the firm may not succeed.

Solo and small practice might be for you as a new law school graduate if you have an entrepreneurial spirit, want to live in a smaller town, and want to have a balance of work and life outside of work. As a business owner, the day does not end at 5pm, but there is a greater sense of freedom and flexibility.

One commentator says the six characteristics of a successful solo attorney are fearlessness, work ethic, interpersonal skills, imagination/creativity, ability to get work done on time, and natural enthusiasm.[17] Take stock of your strengths and weaknesses. If you have many or all of these characteristics then solo or small practice might be right for you. If the idea of running office yourself is frightening, and you cannot overcome that fear, you might be better off in a large firm or government office.

You can make your personal life as important as your work life when you are running the show. The practice of law does not have to be a "work-until-you-drop" model.[18] As a business owner, you can design your business model to support the lifestyle you want, the level of income you need, and promote your physical and mental health. There is a lot of power in being in control of your time, the one thing you can never get back.

There are certainly people who should not start their own law firm. People who are not self motivated, averse to risk (such as the risk of your firm failing), and shy may want to stay away from starting a firm.[19] It is not for every attorney.

⚖ *Quotes from the Bar*

"You have to be pretty courageous if you're going to start your own practice, especially if you hadn't practiced law before. I went directly from being a law student to running a solo practice. You have to be courageous to do that. You have to be willing to go along without somebody there directing you on what to do."

– Vince Taylor

"And as the owner of a solo or small firm, if I have a bad year, it's on me. I'm digging into my line of credit to make payroll and pay the bills and advertising and all that. I don't have someone else here to help float the ship. But I wouldn't trade that for the benefits."

– Matt Lloyd

"There are so many challenges to being self-employed with your own office. Perhaps the biggest challenge is the constant stress caused by handling at any one time 50 to 75 clients' problems in addition to all of the challenges and problems you have in your own life."

– Jawn Bauer

Chapter 2: Setting up an Office

📕 *Chapter Highlights*

To Do List for Setting Up an Office

- **Startup Money** – Money for living expenses in the early months as well as the cost of starting an office.

- **Professional Fees** – Certified Public Accountant, bar association dues, and insurance premiums will all need paid.

- **Finding Office Space** – Should you lease or buy a space, enter into an office sharing arrangement, or work as a virtual law practice?

- **Firm Name** – If you are starting a new firm you will need to decide on a name.

- **Technology** – You will need both hardware and software solutions to run a law office.

- **Support Staff** – You will need to decide if your practice can afford support staff and how to go about adding help when you need it.

Setting up a law practice requires setting up an office environment. If you go into an existing small firm, you will have some of the physical and technological infrastructure already in place. Going solo or establishing a small firm from scratch with a few other attorneys will require establishing an office space, set up technology, establish the firm, and consider the need for staff.

Startup Money

You will need some money available to get going. Expenses for office supplies, office furniture, a website, software, and many other needs will arise. Additionally, the firm, like any new business, will need time to start generating an income. You might need three to six months of living expenses saved in the bank so you can afford housing and food before the firm starts to produce a salary for you.[20] For this reason, you do not want to deplete your savings to start the firm, but you also want to have some of your own money invested to motivate you. Your specific situation will vary if you living expenses are low or you have a spouse who can keep the bills paid while you get established.

You will inevitably spend more than you expected and find costs that you never planned for ahead of time. You will need to pay state, federal, and payroll taxes, utilities, parking at the courthouse, postage, and so much more. You need to really take the time to consider, anticipate, and plan for both the expenses you can identify and the unexpected expenses you cannot plan for now. Starting any business is not without costs. A law firm is no different.

Professional Fees

After the expense of law school and the bar exam, the fees do not stop. As you begin practice, you will need to be ready to pay for continuing legal education and bar memberships. You may need an attorney and a certified public accountant to setup your business as a partnership or some form of limited liability entity. You will also need insurance.

Insurance will include malpractice insurance to cover your use of the law license to serve clients. As a business owner you will likely want a business owner's policy that includes coverage for items such as general liability for your office space, commercial property insurance, and business interruption or business income insurance.[21] Malpractice and business owner insurance should be viewed as essential elements of running a practice for most people. Other types of insurance to consider commercial umbrella insurance, computer and media insurance, data breach insurance, business auto insurance, personal health insurance, disability insurance – this sounds like an overwhelming amount of insurance needed to run a practice.[22] Find an insurance agent for help. You may not need every form of coverage listed here. Your specific situation will dictate what coverage is most important.

Finding Office Space

Joining an existing firm will hopefully come with available office space for you. If you are going to practice as a solo or start a new firm with other attorneys, you will need to find office space. Some options include getting your own leased or owned office, finding an office sharing arrangement, or working virtually.

Leased or Owned Office Space

The leading reasons to find your own space are the control you have over location and office setup and the prestige of having your own brick and mortar location with your name on the door. You can choose the setup, the size of the office, the layout, and the style of decoration.

Finding and outfitting an office space is no simple task. Some estimates say a firm can be started with $3,000 although it is more common to have between $5,000 to $15,000 to get off the ground.[23] If you choose to start from a blank slate by leasing or buying your own office, you will need everything from the floors up. Think about any professional office you have been in and you can imagine what you need – a desk and chair for you and chairs for clients at a minimum. You may need a workstation for support staff or interns. You will need computers for each person. Even in the world of e-filing, you might need a printer and copy machine, or at least a scanner for when your clients bring in paperwork.

If you need it for your office, you handle buying it. You are responsible for outfitting the office in addition to paying the rent or mortgage and utilities such as internet, phone, and electricity. Your office will also need a sign out front in the yard or on the façade as well as a name on the door. These little touches add up and quickly eat into your startup money.

Office Sharing Arrangement

An office sharing arrangement means practicing in a shared office space with other attorneys. Practicing in a "law suite" allows multiple lawyers to share a large office with common use of a photocopier, support staff, and other resources to reduce costs.[24] Being around other attorneys may bring in referrals from those lawyers or allow for free sharing when you refer to the other lawyers in the suite. "For the new attorney it is important to be near other lawyers who can help with advice on how to handle new cases or clients that the new lawyer is encountering for the first time."[25] A brick and mortar office can generate more income than working out of your house and the other attorneys can give you advice on how to navigate the ups and downs and manage the stress of getting started in the practice of law.[26]

Steven Douglas discussed sharing an office:

> Sometimes, maybe a strategic partnership
> would work for you, as a compliment to the
> areas you practice in. One of the big
> considerations is dividing the expenses. You
> need to work out some type of an agreement.
> Maybe it's just an office share where you are not
> affiliated in any way, you simply share the
> office space and split costs.

An office sharing arrangement does come with downsides. You may not want to share an office with lawyers who are your competitors. When a prospective client calls or walks in the front door for the first time in search of an attorney, anyone else doing the same type of law might get the client instead of you. Without a partnership or firm, you will not benefit from that work, you will simply lose out. There is also a possibility to have an inconsistent practice mix, indifferent receptionist, night access issues, and lack of decoration in the office space.[27] Some of these issues are mitigated by newer technologies, such as the ability to run a paperless law office and work from the cloud reducing the need to access paper files.[28]

Office sharing arrangements also raise possible ethical concerns if you seek advice from other attorneys in the shared space. Under Rule 1.6, lawyers who are in an office sharing arrangement but are not actually part of a firm with the other lawyers in the space cannot disclose client confidences to the other lawyers without the informed consent of the client, the disclosure being impliedly authorized, or the disclosure is allowed under the rule.

🔨 *Rules of Professional Conduct*

"Lawyers in a firm may, in the course of the firm's practice, disclose to each other information relating to a client of the firm, unless the client has instructed that particular information be confined to specified lawyers."

Model Rules of Professional Conduct, Rule 1.6, Comment 5

This does not mean lawyers in an office sharing arrangement cannot talk to each other. Rule 1.6, Comment 4, allows for a lawyer to use a hypothetical when discussing the representation with someone else if there is "no reasonable likelihood that the listener will be able to ascertain the identity of the client or the situation involved." Lawyers are encouraged to seek help to best serve their clients. You just need to be careful in an office sharing arrangement to avoid an improper disclosure and running afoul of ethical rules.

Virtual Law Office

A virtual law office foregoes the standard concept of a brick and mortar office to work remotely in the cloud from wherever you are, whether you choose to work from home, a coffee shop, or even on the road traveling. The benefits of working remotely are partly that if you set up the right type of practice you can work from anywhere with an internet connection, and another part is the cost savings by not having the expense of opening, furnishing, and maintaining a physical office location. As Catherine Stafford said, "If I were starting off from scratch today as a solo, I would be a virtual law practice. I would meet with people in a co-work situation in a shared conference room, and I would do everything else without overhead."

A solo attorney with no staff who has the personal motivation to work remotely could save a lot of money on startup expenses and recurring monthly expenses. After the 2020 work from home experience for many in the world, you probably know if you can handle a virtual law office setup. Some of the important aspects of a virtual law office are having a good video conferencing setup (camera, lighting, professional setting behind you), secure client file storage online, and a reliable internet connection.[29]

An American Bar Association survey of lawyers practicing law in virtual firms mentions a great benefit in cutting costs and removing the commute time, but says there can be a steep learning curve to setting up a virtual office.[30] One lawyer pointed out that there are certain states with "bona fide office requirements," so you need to check the rules in your particular jurisdiction about going entirely online. A virtual law office is not the same as a traditional office, so you have to think about it in a different way. You can focus on cutting costs, serving the clients, and thinking outside of the traditional office model. Leveraging technology to automate your workflow and create an efficient process with the proper software can save time and money for you and the client.

⚖ *Quotes from the Bar*

"I would avoid all possible office and rent, permanent overhead, for at least the first year or two. If at that point, I was starting to get more established, I would then and only then consider a permanent office space and possibly some support staff. I know a few people who have started that way and eventually want the prestige of having their own location. But if I were starting off today, I would absolutely not have my own location."

– Catherine Stafford

Firm Name

What's in a name? A young lawyer going solo or starting a firm with others will need to name the new firm. Law firm names have a lot of options, the most common typically involve the name of the solo practitioner or the last names of the named partners in the firm. Some lawyers use a trade name. There are a couple of ethical rules to consider.

The Indiana Rules of Professional Conduct excerpted above place restrictions on firm names that focus on making a proper representation to the public and potential clients. The Model Rules of Professional Conduct previously mirrored the Indiana rules until a change in late 2018 that overhauled many of the advertising rules for lawyers. The Model Rules are just that, a model. The actual rules of your jurisdiction will control and you should be familiar with those specific rules.

Rules such as Indiana's Rule 7.5 will be important for anyone in an office sharing arrangement to be mindful of, in a state such as Indiana that still carries the language about not naming a firm to suggest lawyers practice together if they do not. Simply put, you cannot pretend to be something you are not that will mislead the public about your legal services or office arrangement.

⚖ *Rules of Professional Conduct*

"[L]awyers sharing office facilities, but who are not in fact associated with each other in a law firm, may not denominate themselves as, for example, "Smith and Jones," for that title suggests that they are practicing law together in a firm."

Indiana Rules of Professional Conduct, Rule 7.5, Comment 2

"A trade name may be used by a lawyer in private practice subject to the following requirements: (i) the name shall not imply a connection with a government agency or with a public or charitable legal services organization and shall not otherwise violate Rule 7.1. . . ."

Indiana Rules of Professional Conduct, Rule 7.5(a)(4)

"A lawyer shall not make a false or misleading communication about the lawyer or the lawyer's services."

Indiana Rules of Professional Conduct, Rule 7.1

Technology in Practice

Any law office, whether leased or owned, shared space, or virtual, will need some basic technology to get your work done. That is an obvious statement, of course. You will need both hardware and software solutions to help the office run smoothly.

Hardware

The basic hardware you will need are a computer, scanner, printer, and back up hard drive.[31] There are a lot of options for computers. If you plan to work remotely at all or take a computer to court to work without paper files, then a laptop is a great choice. Many lawyers and judges also use tablets to access files on the go. As Matt Lloyd says, "I don't mind if I can have flexibility and be at home and do a little work with the laptop or on my phone by email, or answer questions with staff. It's a huge benefit. I love it." Even in a digital world, there is still a need for paper. Your best bet is to get the fastest scanner and printer you can afford. Waiting for documents to process through a machine will become an annoyance.

A backup hard drive is necessary because you are working with large volumes of important client information and your own attorney work product. You cannot afford to lose case files or client papers. Proper data backup follows a "3-2-1 backup" plan.[32] The 3-2-1 backup plan says that you should keep three copies of the data on at least two different types of storage medium and at least one is located off site. For example, you might have the original data on your computer hard drive, a second copy on the backup drive, and a third copy in the cloud. The hard drives and cloud storage will represent two different storage mediums, with the cloud storage located off site at the cloud storage company's server site. As one tech site puts it, "You can either tear out your hair when a disaster strikes your hard drive or you can prepare for it ahead of time, but data loss is as inevitable as death and taxes."[33] Services you have heard of such as Google Drive, OneDrive, and Dropbox can provide cloud storage and sync your files online. A full scale online backup service works a bit differently. These backup services encrypt and sync your hard drive and allow you to restore your entire computer from anywhere.[34] If you use Apple computers, the Time Machine feature for backing up a computer works in this way.

If you have partners and support staff, you will need to think about shared servers, network printers, WiFi, and desk phones for the office Keeping everyone connected seamlessly across computers is a bigger task than buying a single laptop.

Software

You will need all the basics, such as word processing, spreadsheets, email, and an address book. Some of the leading options are Microsoft Office and Google Apps for Work. In a solo or small practice, you may also want to consider practice management software and accounting software. Practice management software is by no means a requirement and many small practices do not use specific products such as Clio or Rocket Matter, instead opting for the features of Microsoft and Google to get the job done. You or your firm will need to track income and expenses. QuickBooks is the industry standard for most small businesses, although alternatives such as Xero are great options as well.[35] Proper accounting software will make tax time much easier for you and your accountant.

⚖ *Rules of Professional Conduct*

"To maintain the requisite knowledge and skill, a lawyer should keep abreast of changes in the law and its practice, including the benefits and risks associated with relevant technology. . . "

Model Rules of Professional Conduct, Rule 1.1, Comment 8

Technology plays a vital role in every law firm, especially as many courts across the country move to e-filing and a digital world. Lawyers have an ethical obligation to stay up to date with new and changing technologies in order to maintain their competence. Simply put, technology has changed the practice of law, but many view it as a change for the better. No more long hours in the library and the ability to take your practice on the road with you away from the office.

⚖️ *Quotes from the Bar*

"In the digital world we're in now, people like the immediate gratification of text messages and one day shipping and all these things in the world now lead people to expect things done fast and to get responses quickly. Email lets us do that if there isn't some big research component involved in a question. I think it's great because it lets me do work when I'm at home, on my lawn mower for example, I can stop and respond to emails from home, from anywhere in the world. So yes, it is kind of a ball and chain attached to you at all times, but only if you let it get to that point."

– Matt Lloyd

Support Staff

If you are joining an existing small firm and receiving a salary you may not have to worry about staff hiring and expenses right away. If you join as a partner, form a new firm, or go into an office sharing arrangement, you might have to work with staff that you help manage and share the cost of salary and benefits. Catherine Stafford offered advice on how to use part time staff and interns to scale up as your firm grows rather than diving right into full time staff:

> I would always encourage a new attorney to scale that up gradually. Instead of adding a full time person with benefits in year one, get a part time law student or undergraduate to come in for 10 hours a week, maybe two hours every day, just Monday through Friday, let's say nine to eleven, or something like that. Have that person check your voicemail and return things and schedule things and check your e-filing queues. And then if that works, and you're doing well, and you can afford that and you start to get busy again and you start to get stressed, consider four hours a day and scale up that way.

When attorney Matt Lloyd started in his father's law practice, he was not allowed to use the staff for any of his work needs initially. His father told him, "You need to learn how to do it, so you're going to do the job that your legal assistant would otherwise do." It is much easier to hire for a job you understand and find the right resources to solve the problem. If you do not understand the need, you cannot get the best deal and keep your costs in line. The key to hiring staff seems to be not overcommitting yourself to high overhead costs with full time support staff until your practice can consistently and fully support the expenses. Often, you get what you pay for with staff, so if you are only willing to pay minimum wage for a paralegal or assistant, you can expect minimum wage experience and skill.[36] Your money can go further with part time staff or hiring for specific projects early in your career.

⚖️ *Quotes from the Bar*

"I would always go with the minimum you need because you can always scale up. But it's really hard to then fire someone once you've hired them. Nobody wants to be in a position of missing payroll."

– Catherine Stafford

"That was a great experience. Now that I am the owner and the boss of everything, it is great to understand the layers of your business instead of not having any idea what each person does back in the back office. I think it helps for you to know everything from the ground up. You need to know the structure of your cases and the work and how that all works."

– Matt Lloyd

If you are a lawyer who serves as a partner or has managerial authority over staff members, you are responsible for the actions of the staff member with respect to the ethical rules of your jurisdiction. A lawyer can violate the ethics rules when support staff act inappropriately. For this reason, it is important to have staff you can trust and proper oversight of the way the office runs.

🔨 *Rules of Professional Conduct*

With respect to a nonlawyer employed or retained by or associated with a lawyer:

(a) a partner, and a lawyer who individually or together with other lawyers possesses comparable managerial authority in a law firm shall make reasonable efforts to ensure that the firm has in effect measures giving reasonable assurance that the person's conduct is compatible with the professional obligations of the lawyer;

(b) a lawyer having direct supervisory authority over the nonlawyer shall make reasonable efforts to ensure that the person's conduct is compatible with the professional obligations of the lawyer; and

(c) a lawyer shall be responsible for conduct of such a person that would be a violation of the Rules of Professional Conduct if engaged in by a lawyer if:

(1) the lawyer orders or, with the knowledge of the specific conduct, ratifies the conduct involved; or

(2) the lawyer is a partner or has comparable managerial authority in the law firm in which the person is employed, or has direct supervisory authority over the person, and knows of the conduct at a time when its consequences can be avoided or mitigated but fails to take reasonable remedial action.

Model Rules of Professional Conduct, Rule 5.3

Practicing Law

Chapter 3: Promoting Yourself and Finding Work

Chapter Highlights

Important Elements of Promoting Yourself as a Lawyer

- **Reputation** – Your reputation is everything, both in person and online. Small acts can have big impacts on your reputation, particularly when you do not have the anonymity of working at a big firm.

- **Website** – A website is the first time many potential clients learn about you and your practice, so it is important to have a professional appearance online.

- **Advertising** – Advertising is still a hot button issue at times as to whether or not lawyers should be allowed to advertise at all. You will want to determine if advertising is necessary and right for you or a wasteful expense.

- **Family, Friends, and Neighbors** – These are likely to be your earliest clients, but you should also be prepared for people looking to get free advice.

- **Conflicts in a Small Town** – Sometimes in a small town, a solo or small firm attorney

A law firm is not much of a practice without clients. You have to have clients to earn a living. Your reputation in the local community is very important. You will find clients through friends and family, a website, solicitation and referrals, and advertising. You need to think about conflicts, too. One commentator said, "If you think you are too smart or have too high of a GPA to draft a basic estate plan for $300, then you need to re-think your decision to start a law firm."[37] Not every case is the big one. In fact, most cases are not the big one.

The first client you take on will hopefully provide some income, but the real value will be the experience you gain.[38] The early experiences with clients will pay off in spades later in your career as you find your way up the learning curve. "Depending on your life experience and your experiences in law school, you probably need to focus on learning how to be a lawyer."[39]

Reputation

Sophocles, the ancient Greek playwright, is reported to have said, "A man can get a reputation from very small things." The Latin writer Publilius Syrus wrote, "A good reputation is more valuable than money." The English bishop, satirist, and moralist Joseph Hall said, "A reputation once broken may possibly be repaired, but the world will always keep their eyes on the spot where the crack was." For more than two millennia, societies have recognized the importance of a good reputation. As a solo or small firm attorney in a smaller community, a positive reputation as someone who can be trusted and is honest will be vital to your success.

Attorney Matt Lloyd put it this way, "As a solo firm, I'm the face and the name of the firm. I've got to be really careful. If I was in a big firm and we had a thousand clients, one upset client on some little project is not such a big deal to me. My name is not on the letterhead." Attorney Jawn Bauer has found a solid reputation in a small town essential, saying,

In a smaller or solo practice, your reputation is the most important thing that you will ever have with clients, fellow attorneys, and judges as well as those you deal with within the community. You must always be vigilant and guard your reputation with all your efforts. Your word, your civility, and your willingness to care about the people you serve is absolutely vital to your success.

You need a positive reputation both in person in the community and online. Jay Foonberg's influential book about building a law firm said, "A satisfied client is your most likely and probable source of new clients."[40] When that book was written in the 1980s, the source of new clients was referring to referrals by word of mouth. Word of mouth is still important, but the internet has certainly taken on a large role in how clients find legal services. Some studies have shown that more than 80% of potential clients use the internet to look at consumer reviews when trying to find an attorney, 50% of clients look at reviews to assess the quality of the lawyer, and 70% of clients are willing to travel further to see a lawyer with higher reviews and ratings.[41] More than 90% of consumers say online reviews impact buying decisions and around three-quarters of consumers trust online reviews as much as referrals from family and friends.[42]

To keep an unblemished reputation in town, consider the following points[43]:
- Avoid unnecessary debt
- Pay your bills, including co-counsel fees
- Watch your temper and control your social life
- Respect the legal system
- Treat clients professionally and deliver superior service
- Keep your word

Clients need favorable results, but they want to see effort.[44] Clients will pay for your efforts and are more likely to return to you or recommend you to someone else based on how hard you work for them.[45] A lawyer's work might feel routine to the lawyer, but for the client it is likely a big, important moment in their life. A time of uncertainty and concern and they are turning to a lawyer as the expert to help them through the situation. Jay Foonberg says, "I think it's good public relations for you to return calls at night and on Saturdays and Sundays. Tell the client you are concerned about his or her call and didn't want to wait until the next morning or until after the weekend to return it."[46] While little decisions like returning calls at off hours may not damage your reputation if you do not do it, think back to Sophocles who said, "A man can get a reputation from very small things." Repeated small acts are more likely to build and sustain a positive reputation in the community, both in person and online, than any one big action alone. Promoting yourself and finding work starts with building and maintaining a strong positive reputation. Your efforts in other areas will be much more difficult when you have to overcome a bad reputation.

You will also want to build a positive reputation with other attorneys, local agencies, and the judiciary in your community. One commentator cautions that "[b]uilding relationships is more valuable than making a quick buck."[47] If a judge appoints you to handle an estate or represent the interests of a child, or another attorney asks you for some research, be willing to help. Go a step further and be willing to work for free early in your career to gain experience and build relationships.[48] As a new attorney in a solo or small firm, you need experience to become a better attorney. Attorneys with good reputations can often get better deals from prosecutors, more leeway on filings and extensions for judges, and other positive treatment such as court employees taking the word of the attorney without skepticism or needing proof.[49] A young attorney is always being judged by those they interact with as others in the legal field try to decide if you are competent, professional, and pleasant to work with.[50]

Website

Your lawn firm website is one of the first resources a potential client will review in trying to pick the attorney that seems right for them. A website is a way for the client to learn about the lawyer, see what areas of law you practice in, and find the next steps for getting in contact to setup a consultation and hire you to represent them. Resources abound about how to create a user friendly, accessible website and how to show up in search results. At a basic level, a law firm website needs to have pages that at a minimum include a home page, an about page, a biography page, a page listing your services, and a contact page.[51] You are trying to sell yourself and make a good first impression.

Common advice from blogs and commentators suggest actively engaging with social media, setting up referral plans to incentivize clients to recommend you, writing a blog, creating a podcast, and many other marketing tasks. You can find just as many commentators who say you do not need to do these tasks. One article refers to most law firm blogs as "crappy" content that actually lessens the brand of the firm. "You are creating a section of your law firm website that says you know how to talk a lot about nothing. Talking about nothing may have worked for Jerry Seinfeld but this is probably not the brand you want to convey on your website."[52] The secret seems to be that if you are going to do any of these actions like social media, blogging, and podcasting, you need to be passionate about the task and the topic and focus on putting out a high quality product. A basic website that connects the client to you and reflects your work ethic and personality will go much further than a bunch of poorly done social media content that could look very unprofessional.

The Model Rules of Professional Conduct in Rule 1.18(a) state that "a person who consults with a lawyer about the possibility of forming a client-lawyer relationship with respect to a matter is a prospective client." Lawyers have duties to prospective clients with at least some level of client-lawyer relationship forming. This is no different for a solo or small firm lawyer than any other lawyer who meets with a prospective client.

In terms of a website, though, this becomes important to keep in mind to reduce the amount of information you receive from a prospective client visiting your website, whom you have never spoken to in person, that might create a client-lawyer relationship and disqualify you from other representations with other clients. Comment 2 to Rule 1.18 says "advertising in any medium." This includes a website and social media. You may not want to invite open ended narratives and submission of electronic documents from your website with prospective clients to protect your obligations to those individuals and other clients before you can run a conflicts check and decide if you want to engage with this person as a client of your practice.

⚖ *Rules of Professional Conduct*

"A person becomes a prospective client by consulting with a lawyer about the possibility of forming a client-lawyer relationship with respect to a matter. Whether communications, including written, oral, or electronic communications, constitute a consultation depends on the circumstances. For example, a consultation is likely to have occurred if a lawyer, either in person or through the lawyer's advertising in any medium, specifically requests or invites the submission of information about a potential representation without clear and reasonably understandable warnings and cautionary statements that limit the lawyer's obligations, and a person provides information in response."

Model Rules of Professional Conduct, Rule 1.18, Comment 2

<u>Advertising</u>

The approach to promoting yourself as a lawyer changed drastically about four decades ago with the United States Supreme Court decision in *Bates v. State Bar of Arizona*[53]. The *Bates* decision found a rule imposed by the Arizona Supreme Court that prohibited attorneys from advertising to be a violation of the First and Fourteenth Amendments. This opened the door for attorneys to advertise as protected commercial speech. Any advertisement that is false, deceptive, or misleading is subject to restraint by the states, but in general a lawyer may advertise their services.

⚖ *Rules of Professional Conduct*

(a) A lawyer may communicate information regarding the lawyer's services through any media.

. . .

(d) Any communication made under this Rule must include the name and contact information of at least one lawyer or law firm responsible for its content.

Model Rules of Professional Conduct, Rule 7.2

(4) refer clients to another lawyer or a nonlawyer professional pursuant to an agreement not otherwise prohibited under these Rules that provides for the other person to refer clients or customers to the lawyer, if:

    (i) the reciprocal referral agreement is not exclusive; and

    (ii) the client is informed of the existence and nature of the agreement

Model Rules of Professional Conduct, Rule 7.2(b)

The Model Rules of Professional Conduct reflect the fact that lawyers can advertise. The major points are that lawyers can advertise in any media (radio, television, mailing, internet – all included) and that the advertisement needs to include the name and contact information for the lawyer or law firm producing the advertisement.

The Rules contain a couple of additional considerations that may vary from jurisdiction to jurisdiction. In general, a lawyer cannot "compensate, give or promise anything of value to a person for recommending the lawyer's services" except for paying the cost of advertising or a referral service or giving nominal gifts not viewed as compensation for recommending the lawyer.[54] One other exception to recommendations is that a lawyer can enter into a referral agreement with another lawyer or nonlawyer professional if certain criteria are met. The rules seem concerned with truthfulness and transparency to maintain a lawyer's professional judgment and the independence of the lawyer..

✎ *Rules of Professional Conduct*

(e) A division of a fee between lawyers who are not in the same firm may be made only if:

(1) the division is in proportion to the services performed by each lawyer or each lawyer assumes joint responsibility for the representation;

(2) the client agrees to the arrangement, including the share each lawyer will receive, and the agreement is confirmed in writing; and

(3) the total fee is reasonable.

Model Rules of Professional Conduct, Rule 1.5

A lot of lawyers do not advertise beyond a simple website, business cards, and a sign on the front of the office. Others advertise in a variety of ways, from sponsoring events or local teams up to billboards, bus wraps, and television commercials. There are many lawyers who do not think the profession should advertise. As Matt Lloyd put it, "Viewing the practice of law as a profession that shouldn't advertise – I think that's an old timer mindset anymore. I mean, you get doctors that advertise as you drive down the road. Yeah, so I think it's all changed now. . . . I just consider advertising a sunk cost. I have to do it. If I want to compete with these bigger firms I've got to do it and keep my name out there."

The attorney arguing for the disciplined lawyers at the Supreme Court in *Bates* made a compelling argument for the value of legal advertising to the public and helping people find legal representation, saying

> A great number of people in the United States don't know how to find a lawyer, don't have regular contact with lawyers and they also don't have a very good idea, many of them, what lawyers charge for their services, and a good portion of them tend to overestimate the cost of lawyer services.[55]

Access to justice is a major problem today, still, more than 40 years after the *Bates* decision. Many low-income individuals struggle to get into the court system to enforce their legal rights or to have adequate representation when they face a lawsuit or criminal charges.

One lawyer believes advertising lessens the legal profession, saying the lawyers, "they just look like hucksters and it takes away the professionalism of the profession."[56] The lawyer arguing against advertising said to the Court, "The few at this table, this court, the lawyers in this room, the lawyers outside and those who came before us have taken pride in what is good about this profession. May it never be said that this profession was cheapened here in this its highest sanctuary."[57]

Thirty years after the decision in *Bates*, the attorney who argued successfully at the Supreme Court to allow advertising said when asked if advertising cheapens the profession, "My answer to that is: Really the highest duty of the profession is to provide legal services to those who need it and don't have it. When you think about it, the dignity of a profession may not be the highest public goal."

The decision to advertise is up to you and will depend on factors such as your area of practice, the competition in the geographic region, and the general knowledge of your community about the need for and access to a lawyer's services. Just as many lawyers are successful without advertising as there are successful lawyers who advertise. Like everything we have learned while in law school, "It depends." Advertising is not inherently evil or absolutely necessary to the practice of law. Attorneys who advertise are not wrong or damaging the profession, and those who do not advertise are not necessarily the nobility of the profession.

In reality, the decision to advertise or not might simply be driven by the costs. Advertising is not cheap and we live in a saturated market of audio and visual content. One commentator says that for advertising to be effective, you need to have a lot of ads in a variety of places to see a benefit from getting your name out there.[58] Whether you agree with attorneys advertising or not, the cost may not be worth it if you are unable to gain a foothold in the local advertising market, particularly if a high number of attorneys in your same practice area are already advertising as well. Producing and airing high quality advertising will take time, effort, and precious cash for a new attorney in a new firm.

Not all advertising is produced television or radio time or purchasing billboards. In a small practice, think of many of the same small actions that build your reputation as a form of advertising, too. People in the community will get to know you and recognize you around town. How you interact with people outside of your office and the courts advertises the type of person you are to potential clients. A young associate in a big firm will be an obscurity in the broader community, while a small firm attorney can become a fixture in the community. You will want to have high quality business cards and letterhead with a nice design from a good local print shop.[59] You should also consider having your own custom greeting cards or stationery to send thank yous, personal notes, and well wishes for major life events for friends and clients, such as graduations, weddings, and anniversaries.[60] People remember written correspondence more than emails and text messages. You are the product in your law firm.[61]

Family, Friends, and Neighbors

In a small town practice or rural setting as a solo or small practice attorney, "A practice starts with friends, relatives, and professional acquaintances."[62] Some lawyers disagree about representing family and friends. One wrote, "You must remain objective and non-emotional when evaluating a matter for a client. When you undertake to represent a friend or family member, you tend to lose objectivity."[63] In a small town, you likely cannot afford to start a career as a lawyer without your family, friends, and neighbors. "Face reality. You had better satisfy your friends and relatives if you expect to make it as a new lawyer. They will be the source of much, if not most, of your practice your first few years."[64] Attorney Jawn Bauer says small towns are different, and a small legal practice is more like an old school physician than a new-age 9-5 employee.

Taking on these representations may not be easy for several reasons, though. Attorney Matt Lloyd gave the following caution based on his experiences: "Watch out for buddy deals, because people, you know – friends, family, whatever – they can be some of the most difficult clients and most stressful because you're worried even more about doing the right thing. And also, you want to give them a break on what it costs them and it is tough to ask for money."

The major problem lawyers face with friends and family is the expectation of free legal advice. People will ask questions and try to get answers in a variety of settings where it is more informal and easy to have a short conversation outside of the professional setting in the office. Attorney Steven Douglas says, "There is a trick, and this comes with experience, where you're able to look at that person and say, 'You know, yeah, it sounds like you got a real problem. Why don't you give me a call on Monday and let's set up a time and get you in the office?'" Not everyone will follow through and call you at the office. Occasionally you might get asked what it will cost, but you have to be mindful of the fact that you earn your living giving legal advice.

⚖ *Quotes from the Bar*

"Because one of the great pitfalls of being a solo or small firm is friends and family and associates will try to take advantage of that. Some people do it consciously and some people it's just unconscious. But understand that this is how we make our living. And if you're giving away all your services, you're going to go bankrupt. My kids were very much involved for years in high school band and athletics. I could not go to a football game or a baseball game or a band function or anything, where I wouldn't have at least two or three people stop me and say, 'Hey, Steve, you know, I'm here for my five free minutes of legal advice.' And you know, that's a sacrifice that you make."

– Steven Douglas

"I found that there were a lot of people who expected me to comp them because they were friends or family. And what I developed was a policy that I would share with them up front before I started doing any legal work that set out a friends and family discount of 25% off my hourly rate. I told people I have to still charge something because I still have my overhead but I'm happy to give you that discount."

– Catherine Stafford

Conflicts in a Small Town

Conflicts and the ethical rules concerning conflicts are the same for lawyers regardless of the size of firm or location of practice. Lawyers always have an ethical duty to their clients and prospective clients in any setting. You should without a doubt be familiar with the conflict rules for your jurisdiction. What is different in a solo or small firm is that you likely practice in a smaller town and, as mentioned in the prior section, will deal with family, friends, and neighbors on both sides of legal cases.

Judge Catherine Stafford found a novel way to describe when these sorts of close relationships created a conflict that might not be a strict ethical violation but clearly presented a difficult situation. Judge Stafford describes these as "social conflicts of interest" as follows:

> I came up with a way to describe conflicts that I think really helped me. I would have people call and ask me to take a case, and maybe it was a case I was too close to. Maybe it was my next door neighbor. Maybe it was a mutual friend, where I was friends with both parties, and I didn't want to handle their divorce and alienate one side. I would very comfortably say to the person you know, I really appreciate your confidence in my abilities by calling me. I just feel I'm too close to the situation, I view it really is a social conflict of interest.

Another commentator says, "As lawyers, we must never forget that we are providing a service and that we must be worthy of our fee. We generally must establish reasonable boundaries between ourselves and our clients: we should not seek to be intimate friends with our clients, there must be professional distance."[65] This statement seems to go a bit too far, and falls on the side of not representing most people you know. That commentator was further concerned about representing people they might see out in public at the store or a restaurant. That is extremely impractical in a small town and means you will either have no clients or be required to live outside of the town you serve. Judge Stafford seems to have found the better balance, evaluating each case based on the nature of the relationship outside of the lawyer-client relationship and determining if it was just too close.

⚖️ *Quotes from the Bar*

"But I just felt like I was too close to the situation to be a good attorney. And sometimes I would explain that a person who represents him or herself has a fool for a client, and that applies to attorneys as well. And if we're too close to a situation, you don't get the true value of having a lawyer because you need someone who can be objective and tell you when you're wrong. And if I'm too close to a situation, I'm going to have trouble doing that."

– Catherine Stafford

Chapter 4: Financial Aspects of Legal Practice

📕 *Chapter Highlights*

<u>Billing</u>

- **Setting Fees** – Lawyers must charge a reasonable fee, which is based on numerous factors.

- **Trust Accounts and Retainer Fees** – Lawyers are required to use trust accounts to hold unearned client fees, which are often obtained through a retainer fee paid up front for legal services.

- **Collecting From Clients** – Clients may not always pay what they owe you. Collections can be tough.

- **Professional Independence** – A lawyer cannot allow fees to impact professional judgment.

<u>Declining or Ending a Client Relationship</u>

- **Declining Representation** – The best money you never earn might be from the clients you decline.

- **Terminating Client Representation** – Even when terminating representation, a lawyer must protect the interests of the client.

<u>The Cost of Research</u>

- Legal research can be costly if you use commercial database services. There are numerous free options available that will save you and your clients money.

Billing

A solo or small firm attorney handles setting up their fee arrangements with clients and collecting on accounts when work is completed and money is owed. The lawyers who were interviewed for this project had a lot to say about fees and trying to collect from clients, so you will hear a lot from in this section from the experience of the attorneys who have dealt with these issues first hand. One lawyer said,

> As an associate, here's your salary, the firm takes care of the building, you get a salary, and that's all you worry about. In small practice, billing is a difficult problem. In most cases, you'll not bill how much time you have in the case. I mean, I think that most lawyers are going to end up discounting.

Solo and small firms earn their fees in a multitude of ways. Hourly rates are used by 75% of practices, fixed fee in 44%, and contingency fees by 33% of solo and small lawyers.[66] Some lawyers might use one fee structure, although it is not uncommon for a lawyer to use certain fee structures for certain types of cases. Some lawyers find a variety of ways to bring income into the firm. Jawn Bauer described his early years,

> Over the years, I have accepted alternative forms of payment, worked at much less than my going hourly rate, accepted volunteer positions that I knew might lead to future business, served as a judge pro tempore at $25 a day, picked up extra work as an associate professor at a local Community College. I did whatever I could to bring money into my practice in those early years and to gain experience.

No matter the fee structure, you must have a written fee agreement with each client. The fee agreement details the method of billing, what work is covered and what is not, and many other details of payment that will help avoid disputes later.[67] Also, your invoices to the client each billing cycle should give ample detail on the work you have completed. The client is not sitting with you as you work, and as one lawyer said, "you're going to be doing a lot of work that the client doesn't visualize. Part of your job and maintaining the attorney client relationship is to make sure that client knows how much work you've done." As one commentator puts it, "The basic secret in invoicing is to tell the client everything you did. There is no such thing as an invoice that is too long."[68] List the documents reviewed and prepared on the invoice. Keep the client informed by sending them copies of everything you do throughout the month. List the dates you worked on the case and the total hours billed for the month at the bottom so the client can see how much attention their case received.

Setting Fees

Attorney Steven Douglas said, "If your prices are way lower than the people around you, clients are going to ask why. Is this lawyer just not confident? Is he no good? People that are serious about a legal issue are willing to pay for the legal services." Another problem that low fees introduce to your practice is the concern over the caliber of clients it might attract. One attorney said, "If you set your fee too low, you're going to attract a lot of clients who want to pay low fees." These clients will expect the same level of service as a client paying a higher fee. You can quickly become swamped in too much work by underselling yourself. Once you give a quote for your fee to a potential client, you cannot adjust it up if they readily agree, so you will need to learn as you gain experience or talk to other lawyers in the area for help with setting fees, particularly for cases you have not handled before.[69]

🔨 *Rules of Professional Conduct*

A lawyer shall not make an agreement for, charge, or collect an unreasonable fee or an unreasonable amount for expenses.

Model Rules of Professional Conduct, Rule 1.5(a)

Steven Douglas looks at it this way, "You have to understand that legally we're obligated to charge reasonable rates. And everybody thinks when they hear that, that that means low. No, it means based on years of experience, novelty of case, time and effort involved in the representation – you have to figure all that in." Mr. Douglas is referring to Rule 1.5(a) in the Model Rules of Professional Conduct, which is also the language of the rule in his jurisdiction of Indiana for fees. The rule says a lawyer shall not charge an unreasonable fee and lists eight factors to consider in setting a fee. You will want to know the going rate around town to help set your fees. One lawyer said, "This is a fee that depends upon the legal community in which you practice. A fee is a function of where you practice. So you need to be somewhat aware of what others charge." Catherine Stafford says, "My usual advice is get a sense of where the market is and if you're a brand new attorney hit slightly under average." Attorney Jawn Bauer said, "When you are just out of law school on your own you tend to greatly undervalue your services because of your lack of experience. You must always remember that you also have to survive and be able to pay your rent and overhead."

Once you quote a fee or hourly rate, don't back down if the client suggests something else. "What you look upon as an accommodation will be taken as a symbol of overcharging or dishonesty."[70] You should try to get new clients to come into the office rather than quoting fees and giving legal advice over the phone. One commentator says, "Be wary of the 'client' who won't come into the office for an appointment and who is trying to pump you for legal advice by telephone."[71] If the caller refuses to come into the office, you most likely lost a freeloader problem and not an actual client.

⚖️ **Quotes from the Bar**

"You have got to understand what goes into your rate. You have payroll, you've got insurance you're paying. You're charging a rate based on the fact you have a license to practice that is very difficult to get, it takes three years of crazy expensive law school and determination. You have to be focused in a way that most people can't even get through the education to get there or are willing to do the grind of it. When you start thinking about how hard you work, to go to law school, to get through law school, and now you're finally out, you may have student loan debt, whatever. The fees, when put in perspective, are not as high as you might think."

– Matt Lloyd

⚖️ *Quotes from the Bar*

"Whatever you charge per hour, let's say $200 per hour, everybody freaks out when they hear that two hundred bucks an hour. Occasionally I'll do this, if I get a client that really gets frisky, I'll sit down and say, well, you need to understand that I don't get to keep that whole $200."

– Steven Douglas

"There are of course silly things I did, like taking cases where I spent hours and hours on it and didn't make a cent. I had cases where, even though I may have charged somebody something, I ended up maybe making fifteen cents an hour. I mean, you just learn."

– Vince Taylor

Trust Accounts and Retainer Fees

Lawyers are required to use trust accounts to hold client money. Lawyers must not commingle their own money in accounts with the money of clients or third parties.

🔨 *Rules of Professional Conduct*

A lawyer shall deposit into a client trust account legal fees and expenses that have been paid in advance, to be withdrawn by the lawyer only as fees are earned or expenses incurred.

Model Rules of Professional Conduct, Rule 1.15(c)

A lawyer can transfer funds from the trust account to a personal account as they are earned. Many attorneys have stories about not getting the money up front and never seeing it after the fact. Steve Douglas said,

> In most cases, I'm going to demand a retainer up front. I didn't do that when I started and I paid a price for it. Here's the thing that you'll discover: If it's worth it to a person, they'll find a way to pay you. If they're just on a fishing expedition, it's probably somebody you don't want. And I'll go back to something that my mentor told me, "If 20% of the people that are coming into your office aren't leaving, saying that your fees are too high, you're not charging enough."

One attorney suggested working with your current and potential clients when they need some leeway. They said that you do need to be willing to adjust your fees and your collection process based on the client. If the client asks for a different setup, see if you can make it work. The attorney said, "As long as you have an agreement, you know, and they can pay $100 a month or $200 a month or whatever they will agree to, let them pay it over time. That's working with the client. That is part of your freedom in a small firm. You're also showing the client respect."

Abraham Lincoln reportedly said, "The lawyer should always get some part of his fee in advance from the client. In this way the client knows he has a lawyer and the lawyer knows he has a client."[72] Collecting at least some amount up front will also help show which clients may prefer to not pay you. It is better to know who will not pay and avoid taking the case from the start than to find out when the case is over. As one commentator noted, "The same client who would be angry or insulted over paying some money in advance is usually the one who will be angry and insulted over your bill after you have done the work."[73] The type of case and type of client can dictate if and how much money to get up front. A well-known, trusted client or a business client who routinely pays immediately upon receiving an invoice can be billed regularly without major concern. In some areas of law, such as criminal law, the money you get up front may be the only money you get at all, so try to get as much as you can to cover your expected fees.[74]

There are novel approaches to collections and billing that will make managing your practice's cash flow easier. Early in establishing a law practice, just like any business, cash flow will be an issue until the business grows. Catherine Stafford said, "The smartest business decision I ever made was to institute an evergreen trust deposit policy." The gist of an evergreen trust account is that the client deposits a starting balance as a retainer when the legal work begins, then they are responsible for replenishing the account balance every time it hits a minimum amount that is agreed upon.[75] An evergreen trust approach helps manage firm cash flow and increase collection rates on accounts while also allowing the client to retain your services without a large retainer up front. The management of such a system may be more complicated than needed in a small county seat practice where you can accurately estimate the retainer needed for the type of work and where the total cost is lower overall. For instance, a client can likely come up with a $1,500 retainer, but not $30,000 in a bigger practice area in a bigger city.

Some lawyers will start charging a client or prospective client from the first meeting. Many firms refer to this as a consultation fee. You can use a consultation fee to assess how serious a client is about hiring an attorney.[76] A person willing to pay for your time to decide if you are the right attorney for them might be more likely to pay your fees as the case progresses. Some attorneys charge a consultation fee to make up for potential lost income from any conflicts the consultation creates for the attorney.[77] The lost income angle seems more speculative than testing the waters for the client's willingness to pay for legal services and not just get some free advice, but in a small town being conflicted out is not unheard of in this exact situation. Abraham Lincoln said, "A lawyer's time and advice is his stock in trade." Charging for your time is how you earn a living.

⚖ *Quotes from the Bar*

"I very seldom charged for an initial interview with a client. I always thought it was very smart for me to spend some time and not to charge the client therefore not to create a relationship just to dig into it and find out about the case. Then, if I decided not to take the case, I wouldn't be sending a client a bill but say I'm not taking your case."

– Background Source

"For about the first 15 years of my solo practice, I did not charge consultation fees. I thought that I would lose business if I did charge. Over the course of my practice I have changed my attitude. I now most often charge a reasonable consultation fee. This can accomplish much, as it will tell you if the client is serious about consulting with you and possibly retaining you. It also values your time. It helps greatly in the reduction of your overhead expenses over the course of a year by not giving away your time frequently. These fees add up. I believe that if you get the reputation of a willingness to give your advice for free, the phone will ring off the hook, but nobody will retain you."

– Jawn Bauer

Collecting from Clients

Just as a civil judgment in court is only as good as the other side's ability to pay, the amount you bill out of your practice is only giving you income if you can collect on the invoices. Not ever client pays up front for a retainer fee and many times the retainer fee will run out but you cannot just stop working, so a balance due can add up as the case continues. Most attorneys, like most businesses that offer credit, have stories about those who did not pay. As Catherine Stafford put it, "If every client had paid every bill on time from the first day I opened, I would have been rich. That just never happened." Steven Douglas echoed that sentiment, saying, "In the fourteen years I've been in private practice, if I had every nickel that I had been stiffed, I could buy a brand new house and pay cash for it. You know, it wouldn't be a palace, but it sure wouldn't be a shack either."

Even with trust deposits made as retainers in advance, there are still going to be cases that exceed the retainer and collecting additional fees owed might prove difficult. Catherine Stafford brought up the idea of setting your billing rates based on collectability and getting proper retainer fees. Stafford said, "You have to really think about what's going to be your collectability and make sure you are charging enough to cover that and make sure that you're charging high enough trust deposit to cover the inevitable client who then fails to pay at the end of the case."

⚖️ **Quotes from the Bar**

"Now there will be people who will stiff you. That's the ugly side of owning your own practice - you sometimes get left holding the bag and you have to decide whether or not you should let go or whether you feel that you have been wronged by someone who has really cheated you. There are people who simply can't afford to pay. And there are people who just won't pay because they're ornery and think you don't need the money. You have to decide whether or not to sue for the fee or let it go. That's a hard choice in a small town to be the lawyer who starts suing people. You don't want to make it a habit."

– Background Source

Professional Independence

As an attorney, your professional independence is important to protect the client-attorney relationship from influence by outside third parties. A client needs to be able to trust their attorney. In a solo or small firm, there are more opportunities in a small town for situations to arise that could lead to a concern about outside influence on your legal advice.

A lawyer shall not form a partnership with a nonlawyer when any part of the work in the partnership involves the practice of law.[78] If your clients need advice outside of the law, such as accounting work, you can refer them to a CPA or other professional. You just cannot form a partnership to provide all of the services together under one roof. Additionally, a lawyer cannot allow a third party to direct their legal services for the client even if they recommend, employ, or pay the lawyer for those services. The lawyer works for the client, although sometimes it can be tough to determine who the client is. Be mindful of who you owe a duty to as the lawyer.

🔨 *Rules of Professional Conduct*

A lawyer shall not permit a person who recommends, employs, or pays the lawyer to render legal services for another to direct or regulate the lawyer's professional judgment in rendering such legal services.

Model Rules of Professional Conduct, Rule 5.4(c)

Declining or Ending a Client Relationship
Declining Representation

The rules of professional conduct in each jurisdiction will require a lawyer to decline representation of a client when certain scenarios present themselves. For instance, the Model Rules of Professional Conduct do not allow a lawyer to represent a client unless the representation "can be performed competently, promptly, without improper conflict of interest and to completion."[79] In these sorts of circumstances, a lawyer must decline representation to avoid ethical violations or violations of the law, without consideration of the quality of the client or the case.

⚖️ *Rules of Professional Conduct*

(a) Except as stated in paragraph (c), a lawyer shall not represent a client or, where representation has commenced, shall withdraw from the representation of a client if:

> (1) the representation will result in violation of the rules of professional conduct or other law;

> (2) the lawyer's physical or mental condition materially impairs the lawyer's ability to represent the client; or

> (3) the lawyer is discharged.

Model Rules of Professional Conduct, Rule 1.16(a)

Beyond the ethical obligation to decline, there are cases a lawyer may wish to avoid for other reasons. The bad clients you decline to represent "will be the best money you never made."[80] A bad client or stressful case could hamper your ability to provide great service to other clients. In a small firm, your reputation as a responsive, trustworthy, and hardworking attorney is what helps you build a practice and find new clients. You have to learn to say no to the troublesome people who contact you, or, as Attorney Matt Lloyd said, "Because if you don't say no, but you know you need to say no, it ends up biting you at the end." As one commentator puts it,

> Never be afraid to let the client walk who is shopping around or who cannot meet your financial requirements. If the client expresses financial concerns at the outset, it only gets worse as time moves on . . . Taking a bad case

to generate revenue today when your gut tells
you it is a mistake will cost you time and money
in the future.[81]

One lawyer said, "I think if someone has had a history
of not getting along with other lawyers, that definitely is a red
flag." Along those same line, "I don't like clients who badmouth
prior counsel. Worse yet is the client who comes into your
office and tells you that he has filed a formal complaint with
the disciplinary authorities against prior counsel. It's best to
show this client the door after a respectable time. . . I would
recommend that you not charge for this meeting." Matt Lloyd
thinks about potential clients by trying "to figure out, am I
going to be able to make this guy happy?"

A bad client will cost you in ways you might not
imagine ahead of time and in ways that you likely cannot bill
extra for anyway. A bad client might be one who expects to
meet in the evenings or on weekends or has a major personality
conflict with you or your partners and staff that leads to
unnecessary stress and agitation in your life.[82] As Matt Lloyd
says, "You may just want to pass on clients that are really cost
conscious, and they're calling around asking three or four
different lawyers for their hourly rate and they're going to go
with the cheapest." Abraham Lincoln told a new lawyer who
passed the bar, "Young man, it's more important to know what
cases not to take than it is to know the law."[83] A bad client will
never be happy, they will not listen to you, and they will blame
everyone and everything for their problems except themselves,
and will often take their unhappiness out on you.[84]

One commentator says that the most important factor in determining when to decline a case is following their gut. But, if you are not ready to follow your gut yet, some other indicators of a bad client include:

- Calls with an emergency, but does not return your call for days.
- Has called so many lawyers they cannot recall who you are when you get back to them.
- Has what they believe to be a "great case" without providing much detail.
- Does not show up for their initial appointment.
- Tells a different story in your office than they told you over the phone initially.
- Informs you as to what the correct law and legal theory is for the case.[85]

You must try to be objective in reviewing a potential case and a new client. If you allow yourself to be wrapped up in the tale the client is spinning you can easily miss the red flags about a client that will prove more trouble than they are worth in the long run and you might walk into a case with bad facts or a much more complicated set of facts than you realized. As attorney Jawn Bauer puts it,

> There are warning signs that all lawyers should look for when dealing with potential clients. There have been many a famous people who have said that the best clients they have are the ones that they did not take. You do not have to feel as though you must take every person who calls you or comes into your office. Your stress level and mental health will be well-served to

learn early in your career how to differentiate between those clients.

Here are some recommended ways to tell a client no or decline to take a case[86]:

- Tell your client the truth (no merit to case; uneconomical case)
- Suggest alternatives (pro se in small claims, other lawyers, legal aid, public defender)
- Put it in writing (send the person a follow up letter stating what you told them in declining)
- Ask your client for money up front (unwanted clients will go away when you ask for the money)

You may also choose to decline a case because you do not practice in that area of law. While it will be tough to watch money walk out the door in the form of a potential client, if you are not a bankruptcy attorney practicing in federal court, you will not be the right attorney for that client. One commentator thinks a new attorney should focus on one area of law initially, and at most two areas.[87] The reason is that the practice of law is very complex and a new attorney has more they don't know about the profession than they know, so one area of law will be easier to master. A lot of successful attorneys in work in general practice covering multiple areas of the law, and often in a smaller market it can be difficult to focus more narrowly. Get a feel for your local market and what the local bar already has covered to determine what works for you.

⚖️ **Quotes from the Bar**

"I think you should always be careful in choosing your client. I have always thought that the attorney client relationship is a bilateral relationship. Now, the client selects the attorney, everybody knows that. But I also think the attorney should select the client. In other words, I think that no matter where you practice and at what level, you should be willing to do one of two things. One is either to accept or reject employment, decide not to take the case for the client. And two is if you get into a case and there is something that comes up, that makes your relationship with the client incompatible, you should not hesitate to terminate the relationship."

– Background Source

"What I know to be a good case is different from what every person that walks through my door tells me when they think that they have a good case. I think expectations are always something if you can get that out on the table early on, it's going to be a good indicator of whether or not you want to be involved with this client."

– Matt Lloyd

Terminating Client Representation

Rule 1.16(a) establishes when a mandatory withdrawal from representation must occur, this terminating the client representation. Rule 1.16(a)(1) deals with client actions leading to withdrawal, when those actions will result in a violation of the ethical rules or the law (i.e. you know the violation will occur). Rule 1.16(b) focuses on your actions as a lawyer and your condition being deteriorated enough to impair your ability to represent the client. Additionally, a lawyer must withdraw when discharged by the client because "[a] client has a right to discharge a lawyer at any time, with or without cause, subject to liability for payment for the lawyer's services."[88]

Rule 1.16(b) allows for permissive withdrawals from the representation of the client. The guiding rule of a permissive withdrawal is whether "withdrawal can be accomplished without material adverse effect on the interests of the client."[89] Although, a lawyer may withdraw from the representation even if it might have a material adverse effect on the client in circumstances such as the client is taking actions reasonably believed to be criminal or fraudulent, the lawyer finds the acts of the client repugnant or fundamentally disagrees with the acts, or the client makes the representation unreasonably difficult.[90]

Any time you withdraw from the representation of a client, you should prepare a written document with the facts and details of the circumstances leading to the termination. Your best interests are served by a contemporaneous writing that memorializes the withdrawal in case a dispute arises in the future about the circumstances and timing of the withdrawal. The client should be notified in writing as part of the withdrawal.

Additionally, a lawyer is still ethically obligated to protect the interests of the client even at the time of withdrawal. This means giving reasonable notice, allowing time to hire a new attorney, returning the client's property, and refunding any fees paid in advance that were not earned yet.[91] The one exception, the safe harbor built into the rules, is that a "lawyer may retain papers relating to the client to the extent permitted by other law" to hold as security for any fee the client still owes the lawyer.[92]

The Cost of Research

The big, commercial legal research databases can be quite costly to use on a regular basis for your practice. As a small firm, paying for every search, every click, and every case or document adds up. If you do not have highly refined search terms and research skills, the costs may get a bit out of hand. In a small practice, your clients may not be able to or wish to pay for these costs, but you do not want to absorb those costs. Attorney Matt Lloyd described these big databases by saying, "We stopped using Westlaw and Lexus a long time ago because it was so expensive. You'd get on to do some research, print some secondary sources, and then we get, you know, thousand dollar bills in the mail."

There are ways to go about conducting your legal research for free. If you live near a law school, you can access the law library to conduct free research using hard copy books in the collection. A law library may also have free access for the public to some commercial databases as well as law librarians who are typically willing to help direct you to the right resources. Another benefit of practicing law near a law school is that you can find student interns. Matt Lloyd said,

> A great way to bypass all of that is to have interns or law clerks work for you. You can pass off those research assignments and have a memo put together for you. Those services are great in school, but once you're out and you realize, wait, we don't have this, we don't have that. What am I going to do? You have to find workarounds.

Google and Google Scholar are also growing resources for legal research. State statutes, rules of evidence, and other court information is available online free of charge. Many jurisdictions now have cases and court filings available online.

Legal research services such as Casemaker and Fastcase can be accessed through your membership in a state bar association and other associations provide access to research services, such as Trial Smith through the Trial Lawyers Association. Legal research can be expensive, but it does not have to be.

⚖️ *Quotes from the Bar*

"I do not use commercial research databases. I think I'm a better attorney because I don't use those services. I still use the law library. I mean, I know how to use books, I'm really good at using law books. They give you a different perspective on the law than electronic law does. Because with electronic law you just type in some keywords and it takes you where they want you to go. Whereas with regard to books, you can get a general overview of a topic better than you can online. I mean, there's a lot of things that are available for free on the internet. Now, you can almost access any case you want to for free. Those electronic services really aren't necessary."

– Vince Taylor

Chapter 5: Maintaining Your Sanity

Chapter Highlights

Finding Support as You Practice Law

- **Mentors** – a mentor can help you avoid common mistakes attorneys make early in their careers and give you advice on how to grow your practice.

- **Getting Help on Cases** – as a new attorney in a small firm, you will not know everything about practicing law and you may not have someone in the office next door, so you need to be able to ask for help.

Balancing the Workload

- Diligence is required for attorneys and a major consideration for solo and small firm attorneys is to avoid getting in over your head with cases which can lead to procrastination.

Finding Support as You Practice Law

Being an attorney, and particularly a new attorney still learning the ropes, is a stressful venture at times. Lawyers are "reservoirs of disaster" who focus on what can go wrong.[93] Lawyers sell their time and advice, which is difficult to scale up when pressure from clients, opposing counsel, and managing partners build. As one attorney said about the pressure, "They can't make more time. As their workload grows, something has to give. First, it's vacations. Then weekends. Then evenings. Then family and friends."[94] These pressures lead to lawyers being 3.6 times more likely to be depressed than people in other jobs, with one study finding 28% of lawyers suffer from depression and 21% have problems with abusing alcohol.[95]

Attorney Steven Douglas advises new members of the bar to "[h]ave a support group. . . . You need to get away sometimes. Have a group of friends or family that understand that you're going to take your lumps and learn from them, but have a support system there that can say, you know you're doing a great job." Maybe get a dog, too. The goal is to have a network of people so you are not alone. A solo or small practice does not have the built in support staff, social network, fellow associates, and mentors of a bigger firm. You have to work at it a bit more in a small firm. Ultimately, though, it is your responsibility to make your practice successful, even with people cheering you on.[96]

It is also your responsibility to take time to eat well, exercise, and be mindful of your physical and mental health. You need to find a size of law firm, a city to live in, and an area of practice that suits you and gives you the freedom the be happy. Simply working to earn more money with no time to enjoy life will not lead you in a positive direction.

Mentors

A mentor is someone with experience in the area you are entering as a young attorney who can help guide you when you need advice or questions answered. A good mentor will help you avoid some mistakes, teach you valuable lessons, and help you grow your practice successfully. You are the one doing the work and you need to work hard. A mentor can help steer you in the right direction so your efforts are focused in an area that will lead to positive outcomes.

If you are working in a small firm with other attorneys who have more years of experience than you, these attorneys might be valuable mentors. An attorney in your firm, in your area of practice, who has worked in the local legal community for a few years could prove quite helpful. A mentor in this capacity will know about the other firms and attorneys in town as well as how to approach prosecutors and the different judges in your courts.

You may also want to contact your law school.[97] Many career services offices have mentoring programs in place or will at least know where other alumni of your school are practicing, what area of law they practice in, and who has a reputation for being receptive to helping law students and new attorneys. A mentor in a different jurisdiction may not know your local bar, but they can help with questions about law firm management and handling a variety of issues that arise in your cases.

Another organization that will help you find a mentor is a bar association, whether at the local level or state level.[98] Bar associations have a variety of groups such as a young lawyers division, a trial division, or a small practice division. If you get involved with these groups in your local or state bar association, there might be a formal process in place for pairing junior members of the bar with senior members of the bar who take an interest in the newest members of the profession.

Even if the bar does not have a formal mentoring program, you can still find a mentor. When you attend events, hear other lawyers give talks, and read the bar newsletter, keep track of the lawyers who stand out to you and approach someone you admire.[99] Introduce yourself in person or call their office and ask for a meeting or to take them out for coffee and ask some questions. If you have a chance to meet someone, do not hesitate to introduce yourself. You might find a mentor or referral work, or both, from that informal introduction.[100]

Asking questions is a great way to learn. One commentator recommends asking questions about how the mentor makes their decisions or thinks about a case, and avoid simply asking what to do. By asking how instead of what, "This allows you to learn more about their thought process, so you can develop these same decision making skills yourself."[101]

As a solo attorney, one of a few young attorneys starting a new practice, or an associate in a small firm without a mentoring program, you need to take proactive steps to find a mentor. The legal profession is a big, complicated field to take up as a career. You do not have to go about starting your career alone and reinvent the wheel. Find a more experienced attorney and form a relationship that can serve you well for years to come and help you become the attorney you want to be and have the successful practice you desire.

⚖️ *Quotes from the Bar*

"One thing that's really nice about the legal profession is the mentoring. There is a history, I'll call it a tradition, within the profession, that older attorneys mentor younger attorneys, a little bit of advice here or there or a question or whatever. That will help you accelerate your growth as a lawyer. It'll also help you avoid pitfalls. Because if you make mistakes, it takes a long time to correct them. Sometimes it can never be corrected. But if you make a mistake, if you deviate from where you ought to be, it takes you time to get back to where you should be."

– Background Source

"The young lawyer, in solo or small practice should attend as many events as possible that are sponsored by the local bar association. The local bar association is a good place to meet other attorneys. In my experience, they are willing to assist you with advice and guidance. I still call other attorneys that I have developed a relationship with over many years to ask their advice. To an attorney, none of them expect any compensation for their time. I now get calls from other attorneys who ask me for advice. I am happy to try to help them."

– Jawn Bauer

Getting Help on Cases

Attorney Matt Lloyd summed up why you need to get help on cases early in your career as follows, "One thing you do not want to do is don't ask questions. Don't be shy about your ignorance, because going to law school is one thing. But they didn't teach me squat about what it's like when I get out and I'm in a firm and I'm in court and whatnot." The Rules of Professional Conduct have contemplated the need for attorneys to get help and encourages it. A lawyer is required to be competent in the practice of law and this includes knowing when a matter is outside of your current knowledge or skill.

🔨 *Rules of Professional Conduct*

In determining whether a lawyer employs the requisite knowledge and skill in a particular matter, relevant factors include . . . whether it is feasible to refer the matter to, or associate or consult with, a lawyer of established competence in the field in question.

Model Rules of Professional Conduct, Rule 1.1, Comment 1

Attorney Matt Lloyd now practices as a solo attorney. Mr. Lloyd said, "As a solo attorney, not having someone next door to talk to, that's the big thing. . . But I have a lot of people I know, lawyers in town, where I can shoot an email or pick up the phone and call somebody and say, 'Hey, how would you deal with this?' That's one of the biggest drawbacks I think."

Once you have decided you need to ask for some assistance, make sure you understand what you need to ask about. Ask yourself these three questions[102]:

1. Do you need information on one or two issues related to the claim?
2. How much time will you need to discuss your questions?
3. Do you need to be taught a practice area?

These three questions are important because they help you determine what you ask asking the other attorney for when you contact them. Do you need an answer to one question that can be done effectively via email or a phone call, or do you need to sit down for a longer discussion over lunch? You are asking a busy attorney for their time, so be sure to realize it is "good policy to ask the person what they prefer first" before making plans or jumping right into a long email chain or series of phone calls.[103]

You need to be mindful of the limits of asking another attorney for some free advice or expecting ongoing help for the price of a single lunch. For instance, "[i]f you think you need more than a lunch meeting, then you should really consider asking someone to co-counsel or simply refer the case."[104] You might be able to learn more and build a lasting relationship with another lawyer by showing a willingness to share the income and the case with the attorney rather than simply asking for their input and risk running out your welcome.

Although the Rules of Professional Conduct do allow attorneys to ask for help, consult with other attorneys, or refer cases, do not forget your other ethical duties to the client. Under Rule 1.6, attorneys who are not part of a firm with the other attorneys they consult cannot disclose client confidences to the other attorneys without the informed consent of the client, the disclosure being impliedly authorized, or the disclosure is allowed under the rule. If you refer the case or the client agrees to a co-counsel arrangement, the other attorney will be privy to client confidences. Otherwise, you must protect your client's interests even when seeking advice in most cases.

Finally, when seeking advice, think about who is giving you the advice. Seek out experienced and well-respected attorneys with a reputation as someone you can trust. In the legal field, bad advice is often worse than no advice.[105]

Balancing the Workload

As a solo or small firm practitioner, you may not have associates to unload work on and press for deadlines to be met like a partner or senior associate in a big firm can do. When a solo or small firm goes all hands on deck on a case, it often might be just you, or you and one other attorney. One attorney said when you are facing a bigger firm as a solo, "[Y]ou're going to have to make sure you don't get in over your head. Not that you couldn't handle it intellectually, it's just you're not going to have the resources to go toe to toe, you'll be overpowered."

In the Rules of Professional Conduct, a balanced workload is most directly related to an attorney's diligence in practice. Rule 1.3 of the Model Rules of Professional Conduct says, "A lawyer shall act with reasonable diligence and promptness in representing a client." You might associate diligence with the concept of be a "zealous advocate" for your clients. Zeal is important, but what really plays into balancing the workload for a solo or small firm attorney is procrastination. Comment 3 to Rule 1.3 says, "Perhaps no professional shortcoming is more widely resented than procrastination."

The Rules state that, "unreasonable delay can cause a client needless anxiety and undermine confidence in the lawyer's trustworthiness."[106] A new attorney in a solo or small practice really needs to think about balancing their workload, especially when they do not have partners/associates to help as deadlines approach and too many cases are sitting on the desk needing attention. At best, you might upset the client. At worst, you might miss a deadline or run out of time to adequate research to insure your competency in the matter at hand. You might lose a client or create a malpractice claim against yourself.

As a solo or small firm attorney, you are responsible for following the ethics rules. You need to know the rules and make sure you do not run afoul of the rules. There will not be someone in the firm who handles ethics for you. No one is watching to make sure you follow the firm's policies and procedures. Rule 5.1 of the Model Rules requires the partner of a law firm to "make reasonable efforts to ensure that the firm has in effect measures giving reasonable assurance that all lawyers in the firm conform to the Rules of Professional Conduct."

Chapter 6: Selling a Solo or Small Practice

📕 *Chapter Highlights*

Selling a Solo or Small Practice

- **Find a Buyer** – If you have partners in the firm who will continue practicing, a buyout will be easier than trying to sell a solo firm, particularly in a small town.

- **Negotiate a Sales Price** – An attorney is allowed to obtain compensation in the process of selling a law firm once they have a buyer.

- **Notify Clients** – Clients ultimately decide who they retain as an attorney, so there is no guarantee that all clients will continue with the new firm.

- **Follow the Rules** – The ethics rules provide a number of details about the process of selling a law firm that need to be followed closely.

Solo and small practice attorneys can move on from the practice. An attorney may choose to close or sell their law firm. The Ethics rules do have requirements for closing a firm.

🔨 *Rules of Professional Conduct*

A lawyer or a law firm may sell or purchase a law practice, or an area of law practice, including good will, if the following conditions are satisfied:

(a) The seller ceases to engage in the private practice of law, or in the area of practice that has been sold, [in the geographic area] [in the jurisdiction] (a jurisdiction may elect either version) in which the practice has been conducted;

(b) The entire practice, or the entire area of practice, is sold to one or more lawyers or law firms;

(c) The seller gives written notice to each of the seller's clients regarding:

> [the sale, client's right to take their file elsewhere, and details about consent]

(d) The fees charged clients shall not be increased by reason of the sale.

Model Rules of Professional Conduct, Rule 1.17

In this process, the seller has an "obligation to exercise competence in identifying a purchaser qualified to assume the practice."[107] Finding a buyer is not easy, typically. Selling a law firm can take a lot of work. One attorney talked about this challenge as follows:

That's one of the areas that I would say is a concern, especially as attorneys age. It's hard to find somebody who wants to buy a practice or if you don't have a partner, it's hard to decide to retire. Particularly in smaller communities where the number of attorneys is very small, a lot of older attorneys who've had practices for 40 or 50 years, have a large clientele. And there's nobody to take the practice over. And that is a problem.

Once a buyer is identified, "The selling lawyer or firm may obtain compensation for the reasonable value of the practice as may withdrawing partners of law firms."[108] As Judge Catherine Stafford put it, "I wouldn't ever try to close a solo practice in a month or less. Let me put it that way." Judge Stafford sold her practice to another attorney to assume her position on the bench in the local county circuit court. The process took months as Judge Stafford and the buyer made sure they adhered to the Rules of Professional Conduct and the Judicial Code of Conduct as well as giving notice to the clients and determining what each client wanted to do with their ongoing representation and case files.

Conclusion

A solo or small law firm is not for the faint of heart. You must be self-motivated, hard working, and willing to take risks. Often, there might not be someone in the office next door available to teach you how to practice law. The young attorney needs to be ready to learn and seek out mentors and co-counsel and other ways to learn. You will need to be business oriented and willing to handle collections and dealing with difficult clients. There is not a staff to do this for you. No one is providing a desk and computer on your first day. You need startup money to get going. From a professional risk viewpoint, you do not have a safety net.[109] If you make a mistake as a practicing attorney, you can be sued, suspended, or disbarred from practice.[110] As a solo or even small firm attorney, you are largely on your own with no one to review your work and the risks are entirely yours to take.

With risk comes reward. You can choose your colleagues and your clients. Set your office space up however you want to set it up, where you want to be, and work the hours you choose. You will have a life outside of work and can enjoy time with friends, family, pets, and partaking in hobbies or other leisure activities. The income will be there once you get established and can provide a comfortable life for you.

To sum up the solo and small firm life, let's leave it to the local bar to provide some insight:

> Some closing observations: Drive the best car you can afford. Clients notice. Work out of the best office you can afford. Clients notice. Dress with respect for yourself, for the courts, for your clients and for fellow attorneys. They all notice.
> **– Jawn Bauer**

"Nothing at that school can prepare you for dealing with an irate client that is calling you at four in the morning in a nasty divorce with child custody issues or going into court for the first time in a criminal trial and knowing that if you do not succeed your client may be going away for 20 years. . . . 'The law is a people business.'"
– **Steven Douglas**

"When you're choosing a small firm, I call it a smaller gauge practice. Okay, large gauge, small gauge. But it's still important, because you're helping people, and they need your help. I got a lot of satisfaction. The ultimate thing was always how to get paid, but I had a lot of satisfaction in helping clients get through a difficult time or solve a problem. And I think that's important. I think some people have a condescending attitude toward a small town practitioner. But they also don't have the quality of life. You want some personal satisfaction out of your profession."
– **Background Source**

"If I became an attorney to make a lot of money, then I probably would have gone to work for a large law firm."
– **Vince Taylor**

"It's hard to put a price on happiness. Very few lawyers - county seat lawyers we will call them - are going to make the kind of money that an attorney at a major law firm in a big city is

going to make. It is not going to happen, the economics are different. The clients can afford to pay more, they will pay more. The cases are larger. So yeah, I gave up a lot of lifetime income, but I never missed it."
    – Background Source

Hopefully this book has given you, the law student or recent law school graduate, something to think about regarding solo and small practice. If the appeal of a smaller law firm sounds good, then pursue that area of legal practice. You will not be alone and you will find a very welcoming local bar if you are lucky.

And, finally, don't take yourself too seriously[111] –

Q: What do you have if three lawyers are buried up to their necks in cement?

A: Not enough cement.

Q: What's different about a lawyer's word processor?

A: No matter what font you select, it always comes out in fine print.

Q: How many lawyer jokes are there?

A: Only two, The rest are true stories.

Appendix A – Interviews

The following interviews have been edited for length and clarity. Instead of a direct question and answer format, the text is formatted as a transcript that reads more like each attorney is telling you a part of their story from practice.

Interview subjects include:

Matt Lloyd
Attorney at Law, Bloomington, Indiana
Practicing Since: 2003

Steven Douglas
Attorney at Law, Bloomington, Indiana
Practicing Since: 2006

Vince Taylor
Attorney at Law, Bloomington, Indiana
Practicing Since: 1975

Catherine Stafford
Circuit Judge, Monroe County, Indiana

Jawn Bauer
Attorney at Law, Bloomington, Indiana
Practicing Since: 1981

Background Source (No Attribution)
Private Practice & Judicial Experience
Bloomington & Indianapolis, Indiana
Interview Date: February 28, 2020

Small Firm vs. Big Firm

When I left law school, most of my classmates went into large law firms and large cities. I went to law school on the east coast and I enjoyed that experience. It was a fantastic experience. But while I was there, I realized that I was a Midwesterner. I did not want to live in a congested environment. So I had pretty well decided while I was in law school that I wanted to come back to Indiana. That was the first decision in the decision tree, Indiana or not Indiana. And I was offered summer employment with a big firm in Indianapolis. I had a really good summer there. There were about ten of us in our pledge class as summer associates. I was there for about ten weeks. And I worked with a number of senior partners. I worked on litigation, I worked on just basic research. I interviewed witnesses - a wide range of things, and I enjoyed my summer. At the end of the summer, they offered me a position upon graduation in law school. And the offer was excellent. The financial terms were excellent, the salary was excellent, the fringe benefits, everything.

But I didn't accept it right away. I wanted to think about it. Because Bloomington was my home, not Indianapolis. And after thinking about it, I decided that if I was going to return to Indiana, I wanted to come back home. I wanted to come back to Bloomington. I had been raised here. I loved it here. I couldn't think of a more delightful place to live and work. I did not have a grass is greener complex. I didn't want to go to Florida or California or Chicago. So I declined the offer. And a lot of people thought I was crazy because it was one of the two premier law firms in the state. They had their own building on North Meridian downtown.

But I just decided that I didn't want to work in that environment. And the reason was, I had to keep track of every six minutes. And I decided I didn't want to spend my life keeping track of my work day and income in six minute increments. I just wasn't going to do it. In fact, I think I still have the book in which I kept the record of my work and then I would dictate it in and the secretary went in to enter it on the right file. I decided I wasn't going to work in Indianapolis. I wasn't going to work for a large law firm.

I worked in the local government for a few years then went out into private practice. I got my feet on the ground in a small practice with one partner, senior partner. He was 70 years old. I was 25. He was looking for a partner, so he gave me a desk, put my name on the window, right across from the courthouse on the north side of the square. And I started practicing in a two man firm. I did that for five years. Then I went out on my own, in practice by myself for about ten years. I had a partner the last three years before I went on the bench. My career in practice was either as a sole practitioner, which was most of my time, or in a two man partnership.

I can tell you exactly the term that drove me to small practice instead of a big firm: the term is quality of life. Obviously, the way firms were structured then and are similarly structured now, they had two levels, you're either an associate or a partner. If you are an associate, you are on a partnership track. And the typical term as an associate then was about seven years. And if you made the grade there in seven years, then you would be made an offer as a partner. Not all the partners are paid the same, but you are a partner in the firm. So you're either an associate or a partner, and of course for the associates - it was an economic model, the partners made money off the associates. Yes, the associates work very hard and work very long hours. And that was a profitable arrangement for the partners. Yeah. I was a hard worker, I have always been and I worked very, very hard in my practice as a sole practitioner and as a two man partner.

But I was still the master of my fate. And I still had control of my time. And the quality of life was very important to me. That's why I wanted to come back to Bloomington - it was for a quality of life. For me that was a main consideration. And I thought that I would have a better quality of life practicing in a smaller community and being the master of my fate, rather than being part of a larger organization.

The Tradeoffs

Now, what did I give up? I gave up a lot of money. What I gave up was a lot of income. If I had gone with a large firm, I would have made a lot more money. I can tell you that. I don't know how much more. I don't know if it would be five times more or what, but I would have made a whole lot more money. But I wouldn't have been happy. I wouldn't have been happy even though I enjoyed the work that one summer. It's hard to put a price on happiness. Very few lawyers - county seat lawyers we will call them - are going to make the kind of money that an attorney at a major law firm in a big city is going to make. It is not going to happen, the economics are different. The clients can afford to pay more, they will pay more. The cases are larger. So yeah, I gave up a lot of lifetime income, but I never missed it. I never regretted the decision to come back to Bloomington and to practice law. It was a very important decision in my life. I never ever looked back or second guessed it.

Resource Limitations in a Small Firm

I think that some people will look down on a solo practitioner or a small firm practitioner. It all depends on why you're practicing law. If you're practicing law to help people with their problems, you can do that anywhere. And people with small problems need help as much as people with larger problems. Now, clearly, you're not going to be a juggernaut as a solo or small firm practitioner, because you do not have the financial resources, particularly in big time litigation. There were a couple cases I got involved in. One in particular in the United States District Court for the Southern District of Indiana. in which my opponent was a Chicago firm, and they wanted to paper me to death. And every time the fax went off, here came another set of interrogatories, as you know, and they tried to run over me and my partner, overwhelm us because they were this big firm in downtown Chicago. We ultimately prevailed in the trial. But I was beaten up in that case. When I went home at night, I felt like I'd been beaten up because I was being overpowered by a very large law firm. So when you have a small practice, you're going to have to make sure you don't get in over your head. Not that you couldn't handle it intellectually, it's just you're not going to have the resources to go toe to toe, you'll be overpowered.

When you're choosing a small firm, I call it a smaller gauge practice. Okay, large gauge, small gauge. But it's still important, because you're helping people, and they need your help. I got a lot of satisfaction. The ultimate thing was always how to get paid, but I had a lot of satisfaction in helping clients get through a difficult time or solve a problem. And I think that's important. I think some people have a condescending attitude toward a small town practitioner. But they also don't have the quality of life. You want some personal satisfaction out of your profession.

<u>Choosing Clients and Declining Representation</u>

I think you should always be careful in choosing your client. I have always thought that the attorney client relationship is a bilateral relationship. Now, the client selects the attorney, everybody knows that. But I also think the attorney should select the client. In other words, I think that no matter where you practice and at what level, you should be willing to do one of two things. One is either to accept or reject employment, decide not to take the case for the client. And two is if you get into a case and there is something that comes up, that makes your relationship with the client incompatible, you should not hesitate to terminate the relationship. Now you can't leave the client dry. You got to give them notice, help them find another lawyer, but the client relationship should be a mutual undertaking. So the key to practicing law successfully, I think, in any level and in a small community is making sure that you don't accept employment from the wrong clients or accept the wrong client cases.

People come to you with their problems. Most people don't know whether their problem is a legal problem or maybe it has some other important dimension that can't be solved legally. Maybe they have unrealistic expectations about how it ought to be resolved and your ability to resolve it. And so you're the one that after you look at the facts, you can decide whether you can help this person or not. Or does this person have unreasonable expectations that you'll never be able to reach? You may never be able to satisfy this client because this client wants something that you can't provide. Client selection is very important. And in a smaller community, you have a smaller client pool. I never really considered it a problem. I looked at it more as a matter of the case, I didn't look so much at the client. Is the problem something I can resolve, am I capable of doing it? Does this case add merit? Is it a loser? In other words, on the facts of the law can it be solved, or does the client have unrealistic expectations?

I very seldom charged for an initial interview with a client. I always thought it was very smart for me to spend some time and not to charge the client therefore not to create a relationship just to dig into it and find out about the case. Then, if I decided not to take the case, I wouldn't be sending a client a bill but say I'm not taking your case.

I think if someone has had a history of not getting along with other lawyers, that definitely is a red flag. And you don't want to take a case that you look at on the front end as a loser. I mean, some people have problems that you can't solve. In fact, they may be on the wrong side of the case. And of course, as a lawyer, you like to be on the right side of the case. Now, that doesn't mean that you don't want to represent people who are behind the eight ball, who have a difficult case, but you might rather be on the righteous side of the case than on the negative side of the case. I would turn cases away, I tried to do it gently. I don't think this is the case I want or I don't think I can help you.

Billing

As an associate, here's your salary, the firm takes care of the building, you get a salary, and that's all you worry about. In small practice, billing is a difficult problem. In most cases, you'll not bill how much time you have in the case. I mean, I think that most lawyers are going to end up discounting. They're going to use the billable hour as a metric to get in the ballpark. One of the reasons I didn't go with the Indianapolis firm was because I didn't want to keep track of every six minutes. And so I kept track of my time in most cases. I did try with my clients to always describe the work that was done. And I would often have statements that would run for pages in which I would just list in a narrative or serial form what I did with the date right after it. The client could look at this and go through it to see how much work was done. Keeping in mind that even a client of goodwill who expects to pay is not sitting next to you while you do your work. And so as a result, you're going to be doing a lot of work that the client doesn't visualize. Part of your job and maintaining the attorney client relationship is to make sure that client knows how much work you've done. When they got a bill, they saw I did a lot more work than they realized.

Tthe only ethical rule would be to charge an unreasonable fee. It would be unethical to charge an unreasonable fee, to resist the going rate, so to speak. A particular type of legal work should fall in a range, and your fee was twice the maximum of the range, you'd have to say no, why are you charging two times the rate? That would be an unreasonable fee. This is a fee that depends upon the legal community in which you practice. A fee is a function of where you practice. So you need to be somewhat aware of what others charge.

Now there's one other thing that is really important. It's not on the ethical side, but really important. You're saying think about setting your fee. If you set your fee too low, you're going to attract a lot of clients who want to pay low fees. So you've got to set the fee at a place that if you are hired and you accept the work, you are reasonably compensated. Some lawyers, their fee would be so low that they would just have dozens or hundreds of clients and they would always be juggling and all these clients expect the same level of service as a client who pays a regular fee. You don't want to undersell yourself. Of course, the thing is, you can put your toe in the water and see how it feels. And then you can adjust your fee based on how it's going.

You do adjust your fees based on the people you serve. You also can put terms in. In other words, if somebody comes in and says, "Well, I'm willing to pay your fee, and I will. I am employed. But I have limited income, can I make an installment plan?" As long as you have an agreement, you know, and they can pay $100 a month or $200 a month or whatever they will agree to, let them pay it over time. That's working with the client. That is part of your freedom in a small firm. You're also showing the client respect. You say to the client, "Look, I know you have this problem. I want to help you with it. But of course, I need to be compensated for my work.

So let's find a way that you can pay this overtime and I'm compensated."

Now there will be people who will stiff you. That's the ugly side of owning your own practice - you sometimes get left holding the bag and you have to decide whether or not you should let go or whether you feel that you have been wronged by someone who has really cheated you. There are people who simply can't afford to pay. And there are people who just won't pay because they're ornery and think you don't need the money. You have to decide whether or not to sue for the fee or let it go. That's a hard choice in a small town to be the lawyer who starts suing people. You don't want to make it a habit. Reputation is the single most important thing you do.

The best thing you could do for you and your firm is to develop a business clientele. Business clients expect to pay fees, okay? And it's a deductible expense, and they conduct business with you differently. A business client is different than personal clients, because they expect to employ attorneys from time to time, they expect to pay a fee and it's a business expense. So the whole playing field of representing business clients is different than representing personal non-business clients.

Billable Hours

In the large firms, they will have a managing partner or managing member, they may have non-lawyer staff that help them with the billing and practice management. They have a firm budget built on an hourly structure. The budget will assign to each partner and each associate how many billable hours they expect that person to generate. For associates, it's typically in the 1800 to 2200 billable hours a year range, somewhere around there. Now, you may actually do more work, and every attorney does more work, than the billable hours. You might do one and a half times or two times the hours a month. But at the end of the day, billable hours mean hours that after the account has been processed will produce a bill to the client.They build the whole budget for the whole firm, whether it's 50 lawyers or 200 lawyers or 500 lawyers, a whole firm has this matrix. At any point during the year, it can tell them how they're doing. And then at the end of the year, if they've done better, then the partners will get a bonus. And maybe the associates will get a bonus based on how the firm has performed.

When you're in a small practice, you don't need to do any of that. You probably ought to maybe on one eight and a half by eleven sheet figure out how many billable hours you need at your rate in order to generate what you think is a reasonable income. Also, we've talked about nothing but billable hours, there are going to be times when you will take a percentage of a recovery. And that's not done on an hourly basis. If you have a personal injury case, typically, it's a percentage of the settlement or a judgment. Now, some people are so careful. They keep track of their time, even in a contingency fee case to see whether they came out ahead. I was never that precise.

Law as a Profession, not a Business

When I started practicing, the practice of law was clearly more a profession than it was a business. And it was more genteel. When I practiced, I knew every other attorney in town and we'd meet. I never had a whole lot of time for this, but many attorneys would meet for coffee in the back room of a restaurant every day at 10:30. They just sat back there and had coffee and chatted. And it was said that a lot of cases were settled in the back room. It was a quieter time and things were less hurried. Then while I was in practice, and certainly since I've left, the whole pace accelerated and the practice of law became a business. The difficult part of in a small firm is that you have to do both. You have to be the business side, you have to make sure you're making enough money to live on and to meet your obligations and your goals and so forth, while serving your clients.

I never advertised. I had a listing in the in the business section of the phone directory and my name was in bold print. And it might have had attorney at law under it and my business phone number. I had no Yellow Page advertising and no billboards, no buses. The US Supreme Court opinion which authorized lawyer advertising - that was an inflection point in the practice of law. Of course now for everybody advertising and marketing is a big part of the law.

Just to give you some perspective, the way I look at the practice of law, historically, there were three professions: medicine, law, and the clergy. Those are the three professions. In recent times, anybody engaged in a business has hijacked the term profession. So now all realtors are professionals. Roofers are professionals. plumbers are professionals, electricians are professionals. I'm not putting down any of those occupations, but historically there were three professions. So when you're a lawyer, you are in one of the historical professions. The key thing is you have a fiduciary duty. You have people's lives and fortunes in your hands. And you want to do as well for them as you would do if you are the client.

The Legal Community

One thing that's really nice about the legal profession is the mentoring. There is a history, I'll call it a tradition, within the profession, that older attorneys mentor younger attorneys, a little bit of advice here or there or a question or whatever. That will help you accelerate your growth as a lawyer. It'll also help you avoid pitfalls. Because if you make mistakes, it takes a long time to correct them. Sometimes it can never be corrected. But if you make a mistake, if you deviate from where you ought to be, it takes you time to get back to where you should be.

You can't clap with one hand, you have to have somebody to work with on the other side of the case. I know that when I had some attorneys on the other side in cases things went smoothly, even when we were really adversaries, because they were professional. And then other times, I just had a heck of a time because the lawyer was slipping around and wouldn't return calls or was behind on doing what was supposed to be done. I wasn't sure whether they were acting in good faith and it was difficult to manage the case because of the attorney on the other side of the table, so to speak, and then other cases, you know, it was just really easy to do because you're dealing with a professional.

Moving on From Private Practice

When I moved out of private practice, I was really lucky I had a partner, okay. We agreed when I went on the court that we had a certain amount of receivables, we had open files and receivables and we agreed what I would receive. Then he inherited the firm and the clients and then he ultimately merged the firm with his old firm in Indianapolis. So my transition out of practice was fairly easy. I didn't have to close it because I had a partner. That's one of the areas that I would say is a concern, especially as attorneys age. It's hard to find somebody who wants to buy a practice or if you don't have a partner, it's hard to decide to retire. Particularly in smaller communities where the number of attorneys is very small, a lot of older attorneys who've had practices for 40 or 50 years, have a large clientele. And there's nobody to take the practice over. And that is a problem.

I love being on the bench now, it is just fun. But I do not discount or look down at all on my work as an attorney practicing law and taking clients who walk in the door without an appointment. I think helping people get from here to there, providing legal services as a fiduciary, which you are with a client's life and property, is every bit as important as being a judge. So I want you to know, I think that being a good lawyer is a very valuable thing for your clients and for society. The lawyers are really the glue that holds things together.

Matt Lloyd
Lloyd Law, Bloomington, Indiana
Practicing Since: 2003
Interview Date: March 2, 2020

The Benefits of Solo Practice

I started out as an employee, I worked for my dad as an employee of Lloyd Law. That is different as an attorney. Then eventually he retired. And that's been professionally four years ago, but he's been slowing down for a long time before that. And so I've become owner and boss here. That's amazing because instead of needing to put the 40 hours of face time in, now if I want to do something else in the morning, and I don't have court or other stuff going on, I can do it. Flexibility, it cannot be beat. As the owner, it seems like I'm always on email whether I'm here in the office or not, but my flexibility is something I just cannot put a value on, because I have three young kids and that keeps us busy. I can go pick the boys up from school and I can leave here at 3:15 or 3:30 and go do that without worrying about the ramifications or burden.

In the digital world we're in now, people like the immediate gratification of text messages and one day shipping and all these things in the world now lead people to expect things done fast and to get responses quickly. Email lets us do that if there isn't some big research component involved in a question. I think it's great because it lets me do work when I'm at home, on my lawn mower for example, I can stop and respond to emails from home, from anywhere in the world. So yes, it is kind of a ball and chain attached to you at all times, but only if you let it get to that point. I don't mind if I can have flexibility and be at home and do a little work with the laptop or on my phone by email, or answer questions with staff. It's a huge benefit. I love it.

The Challenge of a Solo Practice

As a solo attorney, not having someone next door to talk to, that's the big thing. When dad was here, I always had a sounding board when I was like, "What would I do about this situation?" Or, "I've been told this by defense counsel, and how do we respond?" Now I don't have that in house. But I have a lot of people I know, lawyers in town, where I can shoot an email or pick up the phone and call somebody and say, "Hey, how would you deal with this?" That's one of the biggest drawbacks I think.

I've always thought I have space in this house to rent out a couple of offices. I could bring someone in not only to get rent coming in, but also just to have another lawyer in here. That would be beneficial for both of us to have someone to ask questions and to fill in for each other. I wouldn't want to have a tenant who was a direct competitor in personal injury. But to have them associated, who can help do similar work and be here just for discussions about cases for situations, that would definitely be beneficial. And as the owner of a solo or small firm, if I have a bad year, it's on me. I'm digging into my line of credit to make payroll and pay the bills and advertising and all that. I don't have someone else here to help float the ship. But I wouldn't trade that for the benefits.

As a solo firm, I'm the face and the name of the firm. I've got to be really careful. If I was in a big firm and we had a thousand clients, one upset client on some little project is not such a big deal to me. My name is not on the letterhead. In a small firm, I'm always looking to make a happy client in the end. That's ultimately the goal whether that means through effort, through personal contacts, and always making them feel welcome when they come in, to charging a fair fee and not making them think I've ripped them off in the end.

Comparison to a Big Firm

It kind of depends on the person. I know some people love big firm life – the prestige or whatever. I don't get that. I don't like big cities. I'm kind of a country boy. And so I go home and want to be in the woods away from people for the most part. Big firm means big city to me. I don't want to be in Indianapolis and deal with all that concrete and traffic and all that. All my buddies from law school ended up going that way into big firms. They're kind of all over from Denver, Chicago, DC. And they're doing fine and well, but it's a different kind of career than what my legal career has been. I'm just little me and I run my office in a small community, but a pretty awesome community without IU and everything it offers. So, I think that's the criteria. And a lot of people just need to go work in the trenches, pay off their student debt. Go get the big job at the big firm and put in your 80 hour weeks, get your debt paid off and then the pressure is off a little bit. Then you can really figure out what you want to do and go back to your hometown or a smaller town or a smaller firm.

Starting Your Career

When I first started, dad had me not rely on his staff. He said, "You need to learn how to do it, so you're going to do the job that your legal assistant would otherwise do." So I spent the first year or so doing all my own work. In a personal injury case, for example, I had to get the medical records, and review them and make sure they're related and match up the medical records with the medical bills, because how much medical expenses a client has is directly related to what the case might be worth. And so he wanted me to do all that work so I knew in the future when I had staff to do it for me, what it took and what it was all about. That was a great experience. Now that I am the owner and the boss of everything, it is great to understand the layers of your business instead of not having any idea what each person does back in the back office. I think it helps for you to know everything from the ground up. You need to know the structure of your cases and the work and how that all works.

One thing you do not want to do is don't ask questions. Don't be shy about your ignorance, because going to law school is one thing. But they didn't teach me squat about what it's like when I get out and I'm in a firm and I'm in court and whatnot. All those professors you know, it's all just theoretical and a lot of them haven't even been sleeves rolled up in front of the judge making the arguments or any of that. So that was something I felt ignorant about for a while, I felt like I was beneath the legal systems because they knew the process of things, or this judge likes it this way or whatever. So dad just threw me in the trenches really and said, here's the case, ask questions to figure it out. The staff have been doing this for years so ask them if you have questions. Don't feel bad about it. You're going to feel dumb, you're going to be stressed out because even the simplest things like hearings are new. The first time I went in front of a judge, I was freaked out.

Advertising & Expenses

Viewing the practice of law as a profession that shouldn't advertise – I think that's an old timer mindset anymore. I mean, you get doctors that advertise as you drive down the road. Yeah, so I think it's all changed now. I think back in the day when the rules first changed, there were a few big names out there that jumped on the advertising bandwagon quickly. I think they were looked at by the profession as a snake, profiting on people's misery and injury and death. Anymore? It's so commonplace that I don't think people do have an opinion of it, as long as it's clean advertising, and not classless, slimy advertising. I don't think most have a problem with it. And if they do, I think it's that old view. My dad was the same way when people first were advertising he was like, "Seriously, you can be on the back of phone books now trying to get injury cases?" They used to just sit back and hope a case walked through the door. I think there's probably still some attorneys out there that think lawyers shouldn't really advertise. The public at large, though, I think they're so used to at this point, it is what it is. Generally, look at the area of law you are in, who you are competing against, and as long as you follow the rules and you are ethical it's not a bad thing to advertise.

With advertising expenses, it's almost kind of the reverse of what you might think it was when money's tight and cases aren't coming in. We don't pinch pennies on advertising. We spend more when we think the work is drying up. If I didn't advertise I would get some referral cases from people I know, but not nearly what I would get if I maintain the advertising or increase the advertising. I just consider advertising a sunk cost. I have to do it. If I want to compete with these bigger firms I've got to do it and keep my name out there. My face out there, my logo out there. And so I just consider it a sunk cost. I'm going to spend a given amount this year, about that next year, maybe a little more next year, whatever it is.

Taking Cases

What I know to be a good case is different from what every person that walks through my door tells me when they think that they have a good case. I think expectations are always something if you can get that out on the table early on, it's going to be a good indicator of whether or not you want to be involved with this client. A good example is the guy that comes in with a personal injury case, rear end collision kind of fender bender, soft tissue injury. He tells you how he's got a cousin that got $150,000 from a similar wreck ten years ago. And it's like, okay, this guy thinks his case is worth a ton of money, but he's going to end up with less than $10,000 in medical bills.

Soft tissues are hard to prove. You don't have X-rays showing a snapped bone and the real gritty kind of medical evidence that helps a jury wrap their head around it. I'm never going to be able to make him happy. Maybe I could make $5,000 if I can get him to settle this case, or maybe he's never going to agree to a settlement that any insurance company is going to rationally offer him. And he's going to force you to go to trial on a small case, with a big risk of losing it or getting a small verdict.

So I always try to figure out, am I going to be able to make this guy happy? Because if he's going to be mad at the end, and I'm only going to make a little bit of money, he's going to go leave me a Google review or whatever that says, "This guy is terrible. He didn't work hard for me, I got screwed." You may just want to pass on clients that are really cost conscious, and they're calling around asking three or four different lawyers for their hourly rate and they're going to go with the cheapest. Well, it's going to be hard to make that client happy. I meet the person and try to figure out their expectations and I try to figure out how good the case is. Is it going to be kind of a relatively straightforward situation or do they come with all kinds of baggage that's going to be hard to deal with again, and get along with the staff. There's tons of factors, it's tough. You've got to say, no, go down the road. It's not something I'm comfortable with. Because if you don't say no, but you know you need to say no, it ends up biting you at the end.

Fees

In personal injury, I work on a contingency fee. You've got to get used to that six months of not getting paid or a year of not getting paid or even longer and a longer in a drawn out case. But once you get through that and get established and find a way of dealing with advanced expenses and funding without being paid for it yet, it's a great area of law practice.

As far as collecting fees, you've got to get paid. Watch out for buddy deals, because people, you know – friends, family, whatever – they can be some of the most difficult clients and most stressful because you're worried even more about doing the right thing. And also, you want to give them a break on what it costs them and it is tough to ask for money. So be careful. You have got to understand what goes into your rate. You have payroll, you've got insurance you're paying. You're charging a rate based on the fact you have a license to practice that is very difficult to get, it takes three years of crazy expensive law school and determination. You have to be focused in a way that most people can't even get through the education to get there or are willing to do the grind of it.

When you start thinking about how hard you work, to go to law school, to get through law school, and now you're finally out, you may have student loan debt, whatever. The fees, when put in perspective, are not as high as you might think. But as long as you work hard and you're diligent, I don't feel guilty about charging a hundred and fifty bucks or more an hour as a new associate or as a new attorney. Which is weird because you're probably used to working in jobs that pay ten to fifteen bucks an hour or whatever. But you're on a whole different level once you get out of school and pass the bar and get that license. You can do stuff that a very small handful of people can do.

Research and Other Advice

We stopped using Westlaw and Lexus a long time ago because it was so expensive. You'd get on to do some research, print some secondary sources, and then we get, you know, thousand dollar bills in the mail. Now, I am very different in that I use free sources. First, I'll get on Google and see how far I can get using that, then I can use Trial Smith from the Trial Lawyers Association. I spent a little bit of money to be a part of the Trial Lawyers Association, but it comes with some free software options, which gets you by pretty well. But if I ever had a big case that really requires some very, very particular research, I'd have to go get like a thirty day or six month subscription to Westlaw, but I hate their contracts.

I hate signing into a 36 month Westlaw contract that at a minimum is going to cost me four hundred bucks a month or whatever plus you realize once you get into it, you have to pay extra for all those you find that are a perfect case, but it's Illinois or its a secondary source that I really want. A great way to bypass all of that is to have interns or law clerks work for you. You can pass off those research assignments and have a memo put together for you. Those services are great in school, but once you're out and you realize, wait, we don't have this, we don't have that. What am I going to do? You have to find workarounds.

I always think that having a lot of credit, like blank lines of credit for slow quarters, or half a year when the money's not coming in, is important. I think I've dug into lines of credit pretty deep at times, knowing I've got this big case and it's going to settle, then I can pay it off and be flush again. So yeah, knowing your finances and having some kind of a system to make payroll and not have everything crumble around you when business gets slow for a period helps. That's important to understand. Same if you're going to hang your shingle and go out on your own straight out of law school. How are you going to survive? You are not going to have much in the way of clients for a while. And if you have some contingency fee cases they're not going to pay you for a while. So knowing how you're going to survive in those initial months or years is important to think about.

Steven Douglas
Attorney at Law, Bloomington, Indiana
Practicing Since: 2006
Interview Date: March 5, 2020

Find What is Right For You

The first thing that I would advise a student is do what you think is the best fit for you. I started as a Deputy Prosecutor, and then I went up to the Attorney General's Office for several years, which is actually classified as a big firm. I think at the time we had over 160 attorneys that were scattered throughout the divisions. It is nice to get some benefits and to know that every two weeks checks are going to be deposited into your bank account. When you're talking about firm life, the big thing that you need to understand is they own you. And I use those words very deliberately. I don't know a big firm where if you're a new associate and you're not billing out at 60 hours a week, you're not going to be there two years.

What a lot of people don't understand, and law students don't understand because they really don't teach this in law school, is just because you put in 60 hours doesn't mean that you're going to be billing 60 hours. So you're talking 90 hours minimum to bill out 60 hours. So, you really don't have that much of a life. If a student is thinking, "Well, you know, I'm top 5% or 10% of my class, and I'm going to get hired and I'm going to be making tons of money to start and it's going to be great. I'm going to be a lawyer. I'm going to be in the city. I'm going to have a great nightlife, great social life." You have got another thing coming, okay? You really don't have that much of a life. Then seven years later, maybe the partners vote you as a partner, and you get to assume the liabilities of the firm. They don't tell you about that in law school.

For me, I was raised in a small town in Tennessee. And I like doing business and a small town way. With the AG's office, I went up against big firm attorneys all the time. When the time came for me to make a decision after the AG's office, I could have tested the waters up in Indianapolis. I always wanted to go into business for myself, though. So I started a practice in Bloomington. The best advice which I did not follow immediately was from my accountant, my CPA, who said, "You are no longer an attorney. You are a businessman that sells legal services." This is what we all do. Doctors sell medical services. Now, there may be an intermediary like a healthcare system or hospital, that does all the logistics and the billing and all the administrative stuff. But then they tell the doctor how many patients they have to see a day in and at what rate they have to charge. That is what the big firm life is, in many respects. You're told what to do. You have to do it. You have to perform. And maybe, just maybe, in seven years you get to taste the sweet success of a partnership, but maybe not.

Business models have changed. You know, 30 years ago, if you graduated from law school, you would probably find a job in a firm somewhere. Today, a lot of companies are hiring in house counsel. Another thing that we haven't just heard but it's happening is a lot of these companies that had funds on retainer are starting to wise up to the big firm business model. They're saying, "Hey, look, we're paying partner prices, we expect the partner to do this, not ship it off to an associate." Well, that's causing them to rethink. And in the last few years, they haven't been hiring nearly as much as they once did. Now, you have to ask yourself that question, "What kind of life do I want for me?" Like I said, growing up in a small town, there were things I wanted to do with my kids. I wanted to go to their ball games. I wanted to coach when that opportunity presented itself. I like helping people out in the community. That's just the way I was raised. You don't get that in a big city setting much. The other thing is the personal relationships. You make connections and when you make those connections, you are in a better position to help your client because people are going to come in with service needs that go beyond the legal needs.

You can help solve those problems with the relationships you have built.

What is Different in a Small Firm

The connection to the client is what is different in a small firm in my experience, it is much more personal than it is with a big firm. In a big firm, you might have a client meeting that you've never talked to the client on the phone. You know, the appointment was set up by administrative staff. The first thing that you think when the client walks into your offices is, "What am I getting myself into here?" And you don't have the option to tactfully decline the representation. That's one of the freedoms that you have in a small firm. I don't refuse a lot of cases, but that is because I'm at the point in my solo career now where people kind of know what I do. I don't have to take cases in areas of law I don't handle. I have that option of saying, you know, this really isn't something I deal with and so, here are a couple names of some local practitioners who can help you. That's a tremendous freedom.

The other freedom that you have is the freedom to be yourself to establish your own brand. Now, I'm meeting with you today and what I would call business casual. When I go into court, I'm dressed in a suit and tie. A lot of my clients view it as pretentious if I were to walk in here every day at the office in a three piece suit. So there's a little bit more flexibility to develop your own brand and your own style. The other thing that you do is you form relationships in a way that, in my experience, big firms don't. Big firms do the work and they bill. And they hope and pray that the people come back. I've been in private practice now since leaving the state. This is my fourteenth year. I'm getting clients today that I had fourteen years ago. They're coming back. Clients that I had last year are coming back, and they're referring people to me. I don't do a lot of advertising. I found that that's kind of a waste.

There are only two professions out there that are not laity. And I love to do this to my physician friends, the only two professions that can elevate themselves above laity are the law and the clergy. You have to bear in mind that for hundreds of years or more, a physician might be your barber – somebody who was good with a knife and knew how to bleed people. In a small practice, you still need to have some of that professional sense.

Office Space

To find office space to start, you need to shop around. Being involved in a firm takes an understanding that building a practice requires you to work at it. So in regard to office space, ask around. You know, you obviously have to be careful, just for your reputation. You don't want to work in a rat hole. People do expect something. You can cut corners where you want, but good internet service is a must. You're going to have to put some money into it, but not a lot, you don't have to have the latest and greatest stuff. A lot of new attorneys get themselves into trouble because they'll go out and they'll want the big firm conference room table and all that. Shop around – attorneys that are retiring, a lot of times they just want to clear the office out. You can find some good deals. Sometimes, maybe a strategic partnership would work for you, as a compliment to the areas you practice in. One of the big considerations is dividing the expenses. You need to work out some type of an agreement. Maybe it's just an office share where you are not affiliated in any way, you simply share the office space and split costs.

Advice When Starting Out

The first thing a recent graduate opening a law firm needs to understand is that there's not going to be a line of people. If you decide to throw out a shingle, to expect a line of people waiting at your door, the first day that you open your office, begging for your legal services, that doesn't happen. You're going to have to establish a practice. The old saying used to be, "If you take care of a law practice for 10 years, it will take care of you for the rest of your life." You know, it does work. There's a satisfaction to that, but you need to understand that it doesn't occur overnight.

Point two: You need to get a good team in place. Don't try to do it all yourself. You're an attorney. You're skilled in the law, and need to enlist the services of a CPA. Notice I said CPA, not accounting services, not a tax preparer. Get a CPA because they're bonded and licensed, and they have to undergo continuing education. They're also somewhat trained in litigation in case there is a problem that they can go in and testify on your behalf. And this one is one that I kind of resisted the first year, because you just don't think about it, but you need to get a mentor. I shared office space with a friend of mine, and we bounced things off each other every so often, but I didn't ask him about the personal aspects or nuances of his business.

Also, no attorney should practice without malpractice insurance, period, end of story. It's going to cost you some money. But you need to have it. You also need to hire a good CPA, you're going to be busy enough building a practice, let a tax professional take care of your taxes. You may need some business help to set up a corporate structure. Find out if you think you're going to need secretarial or office help and look at the temp agencies to start with. Find out about paralegal programs in your area. Many community colleges have a paralegal studies program. These people are trained in the basic nature of the law. They've done some drafting. So you're kind of ahead of the game, because legal writing, as you know, is different from other writing.

Learn to Practice Law

I'll sum it up this way: learn how to practice law. This is what I mean: my study partner in law school was the son of a judge who had been on the bench for 30 years. And after we took the bar exam, we were both convinced that we just bombed it. You know, we were stressed out. So his dad calls him up and says, "I know you guys are just emotionally drained. We're going to go on a little golf outing." So we're going to go on a three day outing. So we're on the first tee. And he comes up and says, "I want you to know, I'm proud of you guys. You know, you made it through and everything." Then he said, "Now, you get to learn how to start practicing law."

That just floored me. I didn't say anything but my study partner who was his son did. He said, "What do you think we've been doing these last several years?" And the judge said, "All you've done is pay your dues." Nothing at that school can prepare you for dealing with an irate client that is calling you at four in the morning in a nasty divorce with child custody issues or going into court for the first time in a criminal trial and knowing that if you do not succeed your client may be going away for 20 years. The judge said, "The law is a people business." The longer I've been at now, the more I realize that he's so right. It's not about statutes or court decisions. They form the basis of our services. But it's learning how to deliver those services to the public in a meaningful, compassionate, honest way, so that they understand what their rights are, and what type of things they may be facing, given the decisions they're going to make. That's the tough thing. And that's why mentoring is so important. You know, getting with somebody swallowing your pride a little bit and getting some help. Learning to practice law is not just remembering what law they taught you in law school, but developing the skills to market those services to the public, in a way that lay people can understand and in a way where they appreciate the services that you are rendering.

Fees and Billing

I was talked into going to the solo small firm conference with the Indiana State Bar Association my second year in private practice by a friend. That friend then introduced me to a top notch lawyer during one of the socializing times. I thought, okay, you know, he will just say hi, and we talked for about an hour and a half. And he just started asking me questions. He asked, "How's your practice going?" Well, I can always be better. "Well, tell me what that means." So I told him what it meant. And he said, "Well, what are you charging per hour?" And I told him and he said, "The first thing you're going to do after this conference is over is you're going to go home, and you're going to raise your hourly rates by $25 an hour. And at the turn of the year, you're going to raise them another 25. Okay?" Now, I never imagined somebody would say you're not charging enough, but people pick up on that kind of thing. If your prices are way lower than the people around you, clients are going to ask why. Is this lawyer just not confident? Is he no good? People that are serious about a legal issue are willing to pay for the legal services. Mentors help with little things like that, where having not been in private practice before and just receiving the paycheck I didn't understand.

In the fourteen years I've been in private practice, if I had every nickel that I had been stiffed, I could buy a brand new house and pay cash for it. You know, it wouldn't be a palace, but it sure wouldn't be a shack either. It would be a solid middle class home. And you learn to get around that to where you understand it is a business and you don't expose yourself to that. In most cases, I'm going to demand a retainer up front. I didn't do that when I started and I paid a price for it. Here's the thing that you'll discover: If it's worth it to a person, they'll find a way to pay you. If they're just on a fishing expedition, it's probably somebody you don't want. And I'll go back to something that my mentor told me, "If 20% of the people that are coming into your office aren't leaving, saying that your fees are too high, you're not charging enough."

Whatever you charge per hour, let's say $200 per hour, everybody freaks out when they hear that two hundred bucks an hour. Occasionally I'll do this, if I get a client that really gets frisky, I'll sit down and say, well, you need to understand that I don't get to keep that whole $200. See, I have to pay a light bill. I pay the phone bill and internet. I have to pay insurance – health insurance, malpractice insurance, renter's insurance. I have to pay my staff. I have to pay the government because taxes are coming. So when it gets down to what is left for me, it's still not a bad hourly rate but it is nowhere near two hundred bucks an hour. You have to understand that legally we're obligated to charge reasonable rates. And everybody thinks when they hear that, that that means low. No, it means based on years of experience, novelty of case, time and effort involved in the representation – you have to figure all that in.

If you're talking about developing a solo or small firm, the first thing that I would do is I would put knowledge of law at the very end. Go back to what my accountant told me – understand that you are in business. Because one of the great pitfalls of being a solo or small firm is friends and family and associates will try to take advantage of that. Some people do it consciously and some people it's just unconscious. But understand that this is how we make our living. And if you're giving away all your services, you're going to go bankrupt. My kids were very much involved for years in high school band and athletics. I could not go to a football game or a baseball game or a band function or anything, where I wouldn't have at least two or three people stop me and say, "Hey, Steve, you know, I'm here for my five free minutes of legal advice." And you know, that's a sacrifice that you make.

The old saying is there's a price you pay to the life you choose. Lawyers are high profile, they are professionals. It gets to be exasperating at times. There is a trick, and this comes with experience, where you're able to look at that person and say, "You know, yeah, it sounds like you got a real problem. Why don't you give me a call on Monday and let's set up a time and get you in the office?" You'll occasionally have one brassy enough to say, "Well, you know, is this going to cost me?" Well, every time you go to the doctor, doesn't that cost you? When you go to the dentist doesn't that cost you? When you go to the grocery store, you just walk in there to look at the food, it's going to cost you, right? Some people you actually have to take them by the hand and make them understand this. This is knowledge and experience that I have paid for myself. And you're wanting to access that knowledge. Therefore, there is a fee that goes with it. Now, you're going to have to swallow that sometimes because people call with just a quick question.

Relationships Matter

I also didn't understand the value, at least at the start of a career, of getting out and building relationships within the business community. And within the legal community. Getting involved in bar associations and committees to develop relationships is important. It's a different mindset. Where big firms kind of have that flow of referrals already, you have to kind of work on packaging yourself and selling yourself in a small firm. And the sooner you learn to do that, especially in changing times, because the digital world and the internet has changed the nature of how we do things, the more you do that to start, the easier your transition into breaking even and then making money.

Have a support group. This seems somewhat counterintuitive because it almost sounds like I'm saying devote your life to your practice. You need to get away sometimes. Have a group of friends or family that understand that you're going to take your lumps and learn from them, but have a support system there that can say, you know you're doing a great job.

The other thing that you really want to do is develop a good relationship with the courts and the clerk's office. Now, that's not as easy as it used to be back when we had to take our paperwork into the clerk, and that is one of the reasons I do not like e-file. Years ago, you'd go to the clerk's office, "Oh, Mr. Douglas, good to see you, what do you have for us today?" They would even expedite stuff for you from time to time. You would see the judges and ask how they were doing. Now the thing that does is if your client sees it, it gives the client confidence in you without you saying a thing. We're losing that as we're going more to mediation and even in criminal matters resolution centers, which are being tried all over the country. So, get out and make acquaintances. Go to the functions and bench bar functions are good to go up to introduce yourself. Go to your county and surrounding counties. Send a letter introducing yourself to others in the local bar. Get yourself out there and don't be afraid to ask questions. Lawyers are a prideful lot. But I could have saved myself a little grief the first couple of years I was in private practice if I had just extended the hand because there were hands that would be extended to me. If I had asked for help it would have made things a lot smoother.

Vince Taylor
Attorney at Law, Bloomington, Indiana
Practicing Since: 1975
Interview Date: March 12, 2020

<u>Going Into Solo Practice</u>
     I grew up in a family that had a business and my family worked in the business. Going into practice for myself seemed like a natural thing to do. I didn't really want to go to a large law firm. I didn't really want to go clerk for a judge. I had opportunities to but I just wanted to open up my office and I actually opened an office above the Uptown Cafe downtown Bloomington, that is where I started. There is a bay window right above the restaurant, and that's where I started. And when I started, I rented the office and I started cleaning it up before I even knew if I passed the bar. If I didn't pass the bar, I was going to become a private detective until I passed the bar. I just wanted to do it. So I did it.
     The hardest thing when starting a solo practice is that you have to be prepared to learn everything on your own. You don't have people teaching you things. My most valuable source for learning things when I started practicing was the people that worked in the courts. I had so many secretaries that helped me learn how to practice law. It's like I went through law school and I went through civil procedure, but nobody ever told us you had to enter an appearance in the case when you were an attorney. So the first time I had a case to file, I went to the clerk's office with a complaint filed to sue and they said, "Where's your appearance?" And I said, "What's an appearance?" So they taught me what an appearance was. And so I learned a lot that way. You have to be pretty courageous if you're going to start your own practice, especially if you hadn't practiced law before. I went directly from being a law student to running a solo practice. You have to be courageous to do that. You have to be willing to go along without somebody

there directing you on what to do. That's the biggest difference, I'd say.

The first real case I ever had, there was a law firm around the corner from where I was, and somebody walked in and said, "I've got a jury trial two hours. Will you guys take it for me?" They said, "There's no way in hell we're gonna take that case. What do we do in two hours now? There's a new attorney around the block, he may do it." So he came over and I did a jury trial we won. And so as soon as that happened, I started getting out there, every criminal in town wanted me to represent them. And in practicing criminal law I looked at it as I couldn't trust anybody. I couldn't trust the prosecutors, I couldn't trust the police. I couldn't trust my clients. And it just seemed like a game. And I didn't want to play a game. So I got out of doing criminal work. I started practicing bankruptcy because no one in town was doing that, and I found the federal courts operate on common sense. I liked being in an area of the law that made sense.

Financial Matters

I've never thought of practicing law as a way to make a bunch of money. It just seemed like at the time when I was at a point in my life where I was ready to make a decision about what I was going to do, I might have done anything. But I became an attorney to become an attorney. I mean, if I became an attorney to make a lot of money, then I probably would have gone to work for a large law firm, and I had an opportunity. Before I even graduated, I had an opportunity to. I could have gotten a clerkship with a Supreme Court Judge, but I didn't want to do it. When I went to law school, I went to law school to get out of law school. I didn't go to law school to enjoy law school. I didn't go to law school because I thought it was a great experience to go back to school. I wanted to work. I had been working as a waiter for two years in Boston. I liked working and so I wanted to go to law school, get out as soon as I could, so I could start practicing law and serving people. So that's what I chose to do.

Well, it's hard to say because one thing you have if you go to work for a large firm, you're probably going to be making more money. And there's very little doubt about that. Of course, you're also going to be used when you first start working and you're going to work hours and hours and hours. Not that you can't, you're young and you're energetic, and you can work that many hours and it doesn't really bother you. But you are going to be groomed to fit into an organization and then you have the opportunity to work your way through that organization. And I'm sure you've heard stories about how people go to work for large firms, and then they're there for two or three years and then the firm decides if they want them or not, and if they don't want them then they go off and have to find a job somewhere else.

As you get older, one thing you do learn is you become wiser. I mean, you get an essence of what wisdom is. The older you are, the more aspects of life you see. You see the good sides and you see the bad sides. The more of that you see the wiser you become. There are of course silly things I did, like taking cases where I spent hours and hours on it and didn't make a cent. I had cases where, even though I may have charged somebody something, I ended up maybe making fifteen cents an hour. I mean, you just learn. You just learn.

Historically, the people that ran for judge the most were general practitioners, who were tired of trying to make a living. They wanted to get a paycheck. When you become a judge, you get a paycheck, and you get paid well as a judge. So there's a lot of people that try to become judges just so they don't have to run the business aspect of law. There's a lot of attorneys that aren't good at that. I do a lot of business law, a lot of business related law, and it makes a difference to my clients that I have my own business. I have a sense of what it takes to run a business and business people like to have an attorney that they think has a sense of what it takes to run a business.

Running a Small Firm

I don't know how long I went without staff. I can't remember now. But when I had a day where I could get all my work done in a day, and if that meant I typed at night, I typed at night. I do not use commercial research databases. I think I'm a better attorney because I don't use those services. I still use the law library. I mean, I know how to use books, I'm really good at using law books. They give you a different perspective on the law than electronic law does. Because with electronic law you just type in some keywords and it takes you where they want you to go. Whereas with regard to books, you can get a general overview of a topic better than you can online.

I mean, there's a lot of things that are available for free on the internet. Now, you can almost access any case you want to for free. Those electronic services really aren't necessary. Even just from five years ago, the number of things that were available over the internet, it's probably increased by 500%, if not 1,000% over the last five years. Probably five years ago, you'd actually be able to access some cases but not blanket access to all cases and now you get blanket access to almost any case anywhere. You can go directly to the court system. If you go directly to the courts electronically, you can go into their files. Some are better than others. I'm glad to see that, the companies that helped make law so expensive are no longer making as much money. It makes the law more accessible to general people.

I have never advertised. The reason I became an attorney was because I didn't trust attorneys. I became an attorney because I wanted to protect people from attorneys. So, I never got sucked into advertising. There were many times when I needed money when I wasn't making much money, but I just kept thinking as long as I keep representing people and doing the best job I can, ultimately I'm going to be able to survive and I've always been able to survive.

Advice for Students

I taught at the law school for many years. I taught trial techniques at the Indiana University law school. I would tell my students, who were all third year students and they were all concerned about where they were going to go with their life, if you really want to find a job, you do one of two things: you either decide you want to practice a particular type of law and you're willing to go anywhere to do it, or you decide where you want to be, and if you go there, you're willing to do any kind of law you need to do to survive there. Either one of those can work just fine. Trying to do both is very difficult. And trying to get the ideal job in the ideal location is very difficult, although it can be done. But more people than not, that doesn't happen. If you got out of law school here and you thought, well, I need to find a job.

You could go around and talk to every firm in town and nobody may need anybody then. So it doesn't make any difference whether or not you were the right person, it isn't anything against you. They just don't need to hire anyone. And then who knows in the next month, maybe five of the people you talk to all of a sudden they need an attorney. And if you would have talked to them at that point, you would have already gotten hired. You can go to a town and you can survive. I was a waiter, I put myself through law school, waiting on tables. I continued to work as a waiter for over a year or a year and a half after I started practicing law. As a matter of fact, I waited on a judge and his family one night and saw him in the court the next morning. And he said, "You look awfully familiar." I said, "That's because I waited on you last night at the restaurant." And he thought the service was great. So it didn't hurt me showing up in his courtroom as an attorney.

The other thing I told my students is don't be afraid of the law. We try to make it sound a lot more sophisticated than it actually is. It boils down to common sense. I used to tell my students when you're reading and studying, when you read case law, don't read it as a law case. Read it like you're reading USA Today. Read it like you're reading a newspaper. Use your common sense. Approach it with common sense, don't think there are all these magical hidden concepts in this story. There aren't. It's just a story. Usually the person that wins in the legal case is the person that was right, is the person that was fair, is the person that was good. It doesn't always happen that way. But you can't put aside your common sense to be an attorney. You have to still think "Well, what's right with this and what's wrong with this?" Other people, that's how they look at things, you know, who was the good person and who was the bad person.

If you represent somebody that may be the bad person, you give them the best representation you can under the circumstances, but you don't try to make them into something that they're not. And you don't try to make yourself into something that you're not. When you talk to people, you have to talk to people just like you're sitting around having a beer on a Friday night. That's how you have to talk to judges. You do it respectfully, but you do it sincerely. And you say what you think and you say what you feel because that's what makes a difference.

One thing you're taught to do in law school is to question anything and to make an argument about anything, but that doesn't make you a good attorney. What you do is you try to think of things that other people will understand and will make them feel something about your case. You have to make them feel something about your client. You're not going to be very successful as an attorney if you do that, but a lot of attorneys just try to come across so complicated that people can't even understand because they think it makes them look

119

smart. The law almost always comes down to two people wanting the same thing. There's a fight over who's right and who's wrong. That's what it all comes down to.

Catherine Stafford
Circuit Judge, Monroe County, Indiana
Small Firm Practice, Bloomington, Indiana
Interview Date: March 13, 2020

Picking Your Colleagues and Clients

I think the biggest part of small practice for me was the opportunity to pick my colleagues. I had fantastic coworkers, and that was always my greatest joy. Secondarily, the chance to really decide for myself what areas of law I wanted to practice and who I wanted as clients. There were cases where they'd come in and it was clear it was not going to be a good fit. And as a solo practitioner or as a small firm managing attorney, I had the ability to say, you know what, I'm not going to be a good fit for you. And here's who I recommend, or, you know, go start from scratch, but here's a refund of your consult fee if I felt like that was appropriate. I didn't have to take the case. And that was remarkably freeing.

Quality of Life in Small Practice

As far as quality of life, it was fabulous. For example, when my son was a newborn, my other attorney in my office and I arranged to have an on site daycare at our law firm. She had a girl a little bit older than my son and I had another child later. We were able to agree on an employee to bring in. We had a huge room in the back, that we turned into a nursery. And we jointly hired a person to come in and watch our kids. And we didn't have to pump, we could go back and breastfeed whenever we wanted, and we had our kids right with us. We didn't have to go anywhere else to drop off our kids during the day. And we used that from really birth to kindergarten. And that was fantastic. That opportunity is not something that I have ever heard of a big firm offering. And I really can't imagine why because, frankly, it was the best quality of life decision that I've ever made. Having that right there.

Occasionally, there were problems. Occasionally our caregiver would be sick, and we'd have to find alternate care. But that happens even if you had your kids at another daycare. So it was certainly not inconvenient and really a fantastic opportunity to have my kids right there with me and to be able to, you know, take a break from work for half an hour and go back and play with them. One of my kids needed speech therapy and we were able to arrange that at my office. And if I was free, I could go back and participate in that and if not, my wonderful caregiver would do it. And we were right downtown. So our caregiver could take the kids to Banneker Community Center or to the library or to all sorts of different events happening downtown, and they had a great time.

Billing Decisions & Compromises

The smartest business decision I ever made was to institute an evergreen trust deposit policy. That is where if a client puts $3000 down at the beginning of the case, they have to keep $3000 in their trust throughout the life of their case. So if I dip into it for attorney fees in a given month, they have to replenish that so that there's $3000 by the beginning of the next month. That way, I'm at least, you know, on average a month away from running out of money. A lot of attorneys do it where they'll bill against that trust deposit until it's gone. But then the client doesn't have to replenish it. Well, in month six or seven of representation, which happens quite often in family law, which was my primary practice area, that trust deposit is exhausted, and that's when the client is running out of money. And at that point, you've developed a bond with the client or you're almost done, or you're almost at final hearing, and you really can't professionally get out at that point. Without great hardship to your client, or great hardship to your reputation in the community, and to your own morals, and yet, you don't want to work for free either. So instituting that evergreen trust deposit really, really helped. I would say cash flow is always a huge problem of a solo and small firm until you get established. It's always a challenge.

My best piece of advice is to try to get an MBA as well as your JD, or at least to take some accounting classes and to get a good understanding about how basic accounting works. Certainly, cash flow is always a challenge. If every client had paid every bill on time from the first day I opened, I would have been rich. That just never happened. You have to really think about what's going to be your collectability and make sure you are charging enough to cover that and make sure that you're charging high enough trust deposit to cover the inevitable client who then fails to pay at the end of the case.

Certainly, I did have to make compromises on billing as a small firm in a small community. I found that there were a lot of people who expected me to comp them because they were friends or family. And what I developed was a policy that I would share with them up front before I started doing any legal work that set out a friends and family discount of 25% off my hourly rate. I told people I have to still charge something because I still have my overhead but I'm happy to give you that discount. Does that work for you? And I think every practitioner would be wise to put that in place. And it's really important to put on the bill every month, hey, here's the full amount and here's your discounted amount so they know the true value of what they're getting.

I also found a lot of pressure to do a lot of pro bono work which was my inclination anyway, and which I was okay with, but certainly that can be a difficult pressure if somebody doesn't want to do that. And I also had a big assumption from every single person I know, as I think every attorney does, that you know the answer to every legal question and you're willing to provide it with no other information given for free at any time. And it was impossible to convince people that I don't practice bankruptcy or I don't practice immigration, or I don't know anything about that. It's hard to get out of those conversations gracefully. I think it's wise to adopt a general statement of you know, I've learned that I really can't give legal advice off the cuff without doing a conflict of interest check. So here's my card. Why don't you call me on Monday?

It is up to each attorney to determine what they charge and under the Rules of Professional Conduct they need to look at prevailing rates and your level of expertise and the amount of work required, factors like that. My usual advice is get a sense of where the market is and if you're a brand new attorney hit slightly under average. I would strongly suggest, however, that attorneys consider not doing an hourly rate if at all possible. And for anything that could be done on a flat fee or contingency fee, to do that. And in fact, there's a type of billing called chunk billing where you say, for example, in a family law case, the initial filing and consultation is, you know, $300. If we do discovery that is a flat $500. If we do mediation, that's a flat $2,000. If we do a contested hearing, that's a flat $2,000, something like that. And that would include all the preparation and other work for it. And that gives your client some firm idea of where you are on the case. And it still allows you to charge by the hour for ongoing contacts, like emails and phone. I find that there's such a large variety, some clients are like, no, I don't need to call my lawyer, I'm good. She'll tell me if something's going on. And other clients really need to talk to you almost every day, and you want to be able to bill them in accordance. You don't want to punish the person who never calls you and you want to bill fairly to the person who does call you a lot. Having billing in a way that is rewarding the attorney for being more efficient is really something I think we need to have in the law.

In other words, every time I developed a template for my firm or figured out a way to make my office more efficient, I lost money because I was billing fewer hours. And I don't feel like that's fair. It's also good for the client for me to give them a little bit of the advantage. So I really wish that I had instituted something like that. And I'm really encouraging attorneys to do so. I was on the verge of instituting it when I decided to run for judge and I decided to not make a change to my firm at that point. But I think it gives clients a little bit more predictability and knowing the fees and it gives them a big incentive. If you're in a mediation and you know that if you sign then you don't owe any more in fees. But if you go to final hearing, it's $2000. Well, that's a big incentive. And it allows the attorney to be efficient in their trial prep, to outsource a lot to their paralegal and to be effective, and of course do a good job, but it also gives the attorney some benefit to being efficient.

Office Space Starting a Firm

Frankly, if I were starting off from scratch today as a solo, I would be a virtual law practice. I would meet with people in a co-work situation in a shared conference room, and I would do everything else without overhead. I would have an online receptionist. And I would avoid all possible office and rent, permanent overhead, for at least the first year or two. If at that point, I was starting to get more established, I would then and only then consider a permanent office space and possibly some support staff. I know a few people who have started that way and eventually want the prestige of having their own location. But if I were starting off today, I would absolutely not have my own location. In this town with the number of attorneys we have and the number of new law graduates, it is frankly not that much more expensive to hire a new attorney than a really good paralegal. You have to consider where those are and where you are located. You can bill an attorney out at a much higher rate than you can a paralegal. You've also got to consider are you keeping up on your phone calls and your scheduling? Are you starting to miss court dates and returning phone calls in a way that is making your clients mad? To me, that's a great indication that you need to hire at least some temporary support staff.

I would always encourage a new attorney to scale that up gradually. Instead of adding a full time person with benefits in year one, get a part time law student or undergraduate to come in for 10 hours a week, maybe two hours every day, just Monday through Friday, let's say nine to eleven, or something like that. Have that person check your voicemail and return things and schedule things and check your e-filing queues. And then if that works, and you're doing well, and you can afford that and you start to get busy again and you start to get stressed, consider four hours a day and scale up that way. Maybe if that gets close to full time or that person phases out, maybe then you replace that person with two part timers or one full timer. I would always go with the minimum you need because you can always scale up. But it's really hard to then fire someone once you've hired them. Nobody wants to be in a position of missing payroll.

Conflicts in a Small Town

I grew up in Bloomington where I practiced law, and I know a ton of people here. I always found it to be an advantage. I came up with a way to describe conflicts that I think really helped me. I would have people call and ask me to take a case, and maybe it was a case I was too close to. Maybe it was my next door neighbor. Maybe it was a mutual friend, where I was friends with both parties, and I didn't want to handle their divorce and alienate one side. I would very comfortably say to the person you know, I really appreciate your confidence in my abilities by calling me. I just feel I'm too close to the situation, I view it really is a social conflict of interest. But I would be happy to refer you elsewhere and here's where I would send you. That really helped express appreciation and let them know that it wasn't wrong for them to call me or anything like that. But I just felt like I was too close to the situation to be a good attorney. And sometimes I would explain that a person who represents him or herself has a fool for a client, and that applies to attorneys as well. And if we're too close to a situation, you don't get the true value of having a lawyer because you need someone who can be objective and tell you when you're wrong. And if I'm too close to a situation, I'm going to have trouble doing that.

<u>Leaving Small Practice</u>

Leaving a small practice depends exactly on where you're going. For me, I was hoping to be able to close my firm and take the bench, which of course that happened. But I also had another attorney in my firm who despite my ten years worth of requests had never let me make her a partner. And I asked her, of course, before I told anyone else that I was going to run for judge and asked her if she would like to take over the firm or start her own firm at that point. She indicated that she'd have to think about it. This took her probably six months to make a decision and to plan how she wanted to proceed. And I was very happy to give her that time. She had more than proved her loyalty and intelligence and capabilities. She ended up bringing in another partner and they formed their own firm. And of course, many of our former clients elected to stay with her. But of course, not all did and that's fine. Some had conflicts with her new partner and some had other other issues or different kinds of law they needed. I was able to end my lease on November 30 and her firm started their lease on December 1. So it worked out quite well for us. But it was a process of deciding for ourselves what we were going to do and giving ourselves plenty of time and a to do list and careful study of the rules of professional conduct and the code of judicial conduct to make sure that we put everything in place to keep our clients posted, to give them the final decision on what they wanted to do, and to make sure they could have access to their files and that all information was transmitted appropriately. I wouldn't ever try to close a solo practice in a month or less. Let me put it that way.

Advice for Starting a New Firm

I generally give three pieces of advice to people considering starting their own firm. The first is to read Jay Foonberg's book, How to Start & Build a Law Practice. That's the book I used as the textbook for my class. I think it's excellent. Some of it is out of date. He talks about how you need to have true engraved letterhead. Well, I don't even think you need letterhead. I think you should do everything online and have electronic case files. So I would certainly get that book.

If I were starting a new practice, I would second get extremely involved in my local bar association, because that is a way to meet other attorneys, to get referrals from them, to start learning who does what area of practice so you can make referrals for your clients when they have cases that you can't handle. You want to take care of your clients, even if it's something you don't do, and knowing the network of who's out there and what they do is extremely important. It's also a way to stay involved and have a sense of community. If you're a solo practitioner, having a network of other solos where you can call and say, look, I've got a real ethical thorny question, Can I can I talk you through it without, you know, disclosing any confidences? If you have a few friends you can do that with, you're going to be 100% better off as an attorney than if you're truly just isolated by yourself. So having those colleagues I think is super important.

Third is to really establish a law office management manual. I think that's critical. And I think people who are considering starting a law firm have to do it before they open their doors. And that includes a marketing plan, a business plan, a financial plan, a budget, all those things that you would put into any new business startup. I think it's absolutely essential. You want to know how you're going to handle mail. You want to know how you're going to handle faxes. You want to know how you're going to handle e-filing. You want to design your website, you want to think about how you're going to fund all of this. Writing it all down in a plan is the only way to do it.

Jawn Bauer
Attorney at Law, Bloomington, Indiana
Practicing Since: 1981
Interview Date: May 22, 2020

<u>Working in a Small Firm</u>

I never envisioned myself working for someone else. The primary benefit for me as a solo attorney was to be my own boss. There were additional benefits that flowed from that including scheduling your own time, allowing extra time to raise your family by being able to attend all school activities and sports and events for your children, travel, and enjoying leisure time.

There are so many challenges to being self-employed with your own office. Perhaps the biggest challenge is the constant stress caused by handling at any one time 50 to 75 clients' problems in addition to all of the challenges and problems you have in your own life. Some of the other challenges include time management, knowing how to run the business side of your practice, and hundreds of other details to being a successful solo practitioner.

<u>Attorney's Fees</u>

Another big challenge and stressor in solo practice is learning about attorney's fees. When you are just out of law school on your own you tend to greatly undervalue your services because of your lack of experience. You must always remember that you also have to survive and be able to pay your rent and overhead. Over the years, I have accepted alternative forms of payment, worked at much less than my going hourly rate, accepted volunteer positions that I knew might lead to future business, served as a judge pro tempore at $25 a day, picked up extra work as an associate professor at a local Community College. I did whatever I could to bring money into my practice in those early years and to gain experience.

I also traded for services. What I discovered is that trading for services seldom works. Get a retainer. I have not traded for services for many years. One time I traded a client services for the painting of my small house. Everyday it would seem like it was taking longer and longer. One day I snuck home to check on the client and found my client in the backyard sitting on a cooler in the shade with an associate of his. By the number of empty cans around them they appeared to have consumed many alcoholic beverages. Needless to say, I ended up painting the house.

Advertising & Reputation

I have never been a proponent of advertising for lawyers. I believe that advertising hurts the law profession. It treats it as a business. I have made a rule throughout my years of practice to rely simply on word-of-mouth from former clients and community members, my reputation, and my good service, to obtain clients. Over those years this has saved me a great deal of advertising dollars that I can spend elsewhere. This strategy has still brought me plenty of clients.

n a smaller or solo practice, your reputation is the most important thing that you will ever have with clients, fellow attorneys, and judges as well as those you deal with within the community. You must always be vigilant and guard your reputation with all your efforts. Your word, your civility, and your willingness to care about the people you serve is absolutely vital to your success.

Consultation Fees & Accepting Cases

For about the first 15 years of my solo practice, I did not charge consultation fees. I thought that I would lose business if I did charge. Over the course of my practice I have changed my attitude. I now most often charge a reasonable consultation fee. This can accomplish much, as it will tell you if the client is serious about consulting with you and possibly retaining you. It also values your time. It helps greatly in the reduction of your overhead expenses over the course of a year by not giving away your time frequently. These fees add up. I believe that if you get the reputation of a willingness to give your advice for free, the phone will ring off the hook, but nobody will retain you.

I am upfront with a client who comes to me who wants to use the law for a purpose that may be less than scrupulous. I strongly discourage them from moving forward. I often will refuse to move forward when it makes no sense and is motivated simply by the need for revenge or making the potential client feel better. There are warning signs that all lawyers should look for when dealing with potential clients. There have been many a famous people who have said that the best clients they have are the ones that they did not take. You do not have to feel as though you must take every person who calls you or comes into your office. Your stress level and mental health will be well-served to learn early in your career how to differentiate between those clients.

Advice for Young Attorneys

The young lawyer, in solo or small practice should attend as many events as possible that are sponsored by the local bar association. The local bar association is a good place to meet other attorneys. In my experience, they are willing to assist you with advice and guidance. I still call other attorneys that I have developed a relationship with over many years to ask their advice. To an attorney, none of them expect any compensation for their time. I now get calls from other attorneys who ask me for advice. I am happy to try to help them.

Becoming a solo or small office practitioner is one of the most difficult things that a law student can do. It is much easier to move to a medium or large firm where you are told what to do and you have a great deal of support. Solo practitioners need so many skills to succeed. You must be realistic, optimistic, and maintain a sense of humor as you move forward. The single greatest reward that I have had in my legal career is that I decided to run my own practice.

Some closing observations: Drive the best car you can afford. Clients notice. Work out of the best office you can afford. Clients notice. Dress with respect for yourself, for the courts, for your clients and for fellow attorneys. They all notice.

Appendix B – Data Analysis

National Employment Data – Bureau of the Census

The 2017 North American Industry Classification System (NAICS) provides statistical data about the U.S. Business Economy. The U.S. Department of Commerce Bureau of the Census publishes the data. The 2017 data is the last available survey of employers.

The NAICS code 54111 is for "Offices of Lawyers," which the Bureau of Census defines as:

> This industry comprises offices of legal practitioners known as lawyers or attorneys (i.e., counselors-at-law) primarily engaged in the practice of law. Establishments in this industry may provide expertise in a range or in specific areas of law, such as criminal law, corporate law, family and estate law, patent law, real estate law, or tax law.[112]

The 2017 statistics show an overwhelming majority of law firms in the United States have fewer than five attorneys.

No. Laywers	Firms	Firms %	Lawyers	Lawyers %
Less than 5	123,689	75.5%	205,968	19.4%
5 to 9	23,034	14.1%	149,075	14.0%
10 to 19	9,904	6.0%	131,048	12.3%
20 to 99	5,992	3.7%	228,305	21.5%
100 to 499	900	0.5%	166,419	15.6%
500 or more	206	0.1%	182,914	17.2%
TOTAL	**163,725**	**100.0%**	**1,063,729**	**100.0%**

Table 1 – 2017 NAICS code 54111 – Office of Lawyers

Viewing the data visually, we can see that while 89% of total firms are solo or small firms (under ten attorneys), that represents about a third of total attorneys:

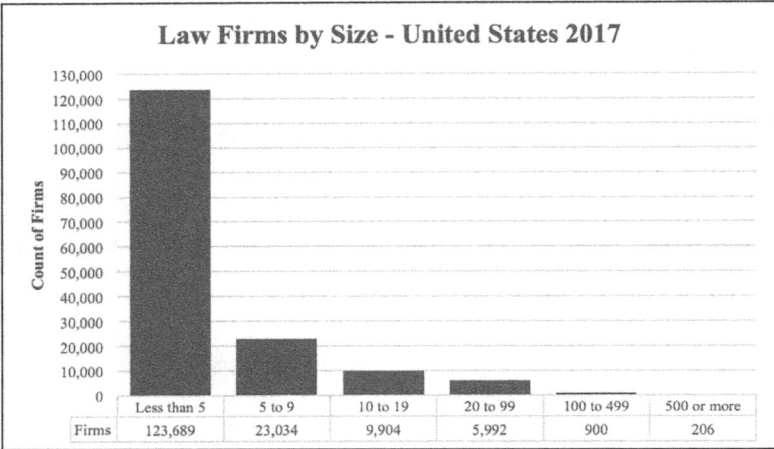

Law Firms by Size - United States 2017

Firms	Less than 5	5 to 9	10 to 19	20 to 99	100 to 499	500 or more
	123,689	23,034	9,904	5,992	900	206

Chart 1 – 2017 NAICS code 54111 – Office of Lawyers

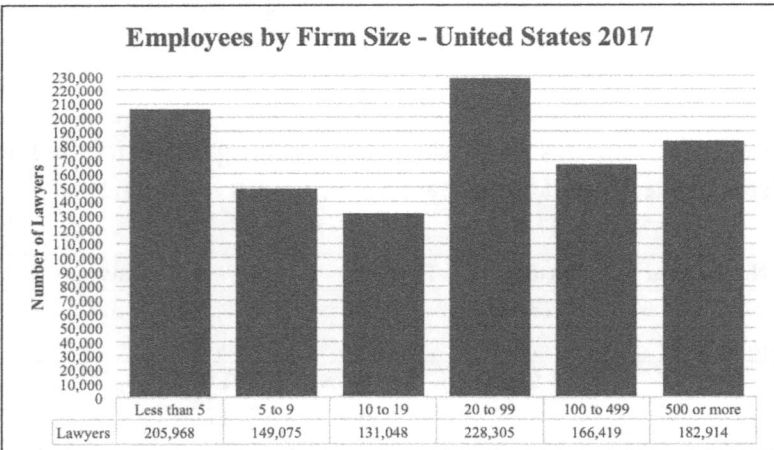

Employees by Firm Size - United States 2017

Lawyers	Less than 5	5 to 9	10 to 19	20 to 99	100 to 499	500 or more
	205,968	149,075	131,048	228,305	166,419	182,914

Chart 2 – 2017 NAICS code 54111 – Office of Lawyers

2018 New Graduate Data – National Association for Law Placement (NALP)

The 2018 data is the most recent report available for new graduates entering the legal profession. For the class of 2018, the statistics for firm jobs and salaries follow.

Graduates in Law Firm Jobs
More than half of law graduates in 2018 went into a law firm as opposed to roles as in-house counsel or in the government. The geography and population density play a role in if graduates go into small firms.[113] For instance, New York sees 13.9% and Washington D.C. sees 7.7% of new graduates go into firms of 1-10 lawyers. In comparison, Alaska is at 100%, North Dakota 77.8%, and Idaho sees 71.1% of graduates go into small firms.

Percent of All Graduates in Firms[114]
- 54.8% of all law graduates went into law firms
    - 1.1% of all graduates became solo practitioners
    - 18.5% of all graduates went into firms of 1-10 lawyers

Percent of Graduates in Firms by Firm Size[115]
- 33.9% of graduates going into law firms were going into firms of 1-10 lawyers
    - This is the largest share of firm jobs by size
    - Firms of 1-10 lawyers were down from 35.3% for the 2017 graduating class.
    - Large firms of 500+ lawyers have been trending up for the past 7 years and account for 29.1% of 2018 graduates going into law firms
    - Large firms were at a 16.2% share in 2011

Percent of Graduates in Firms by Firm Size

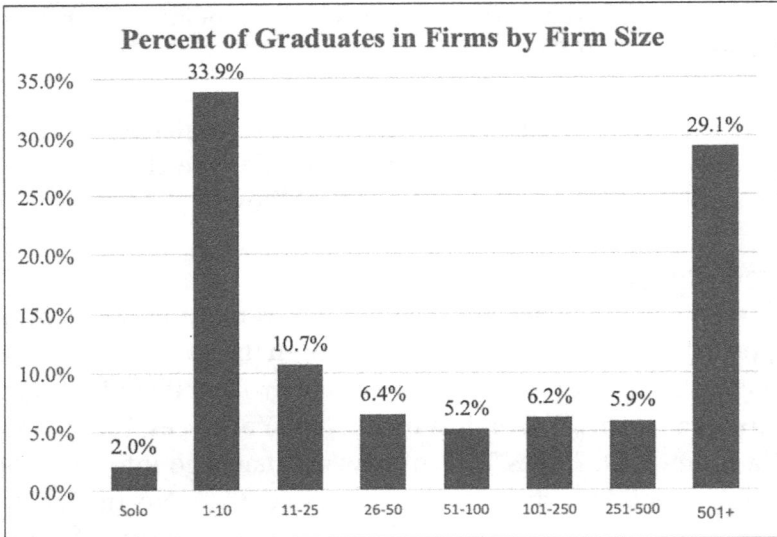

Chart 3 – NALP Class of 2018

How Graduates Find Firm Jobs[116]

Law students find jobs in a wide variety of ways. One way that a lot of students hear about in law school is On Campus Interviews (OCIs). Here is the breakdown of students finding jobs from OCIs by firm size:

Percent of Graduates Employed through OCIs by Firm Size

Firm Size	Percent
1-10	1.4%
11-25	6.5%
26-50	21.4%
51-100	29.9%
101-250	42.3%
251-500	47.7%
501+	61.8%

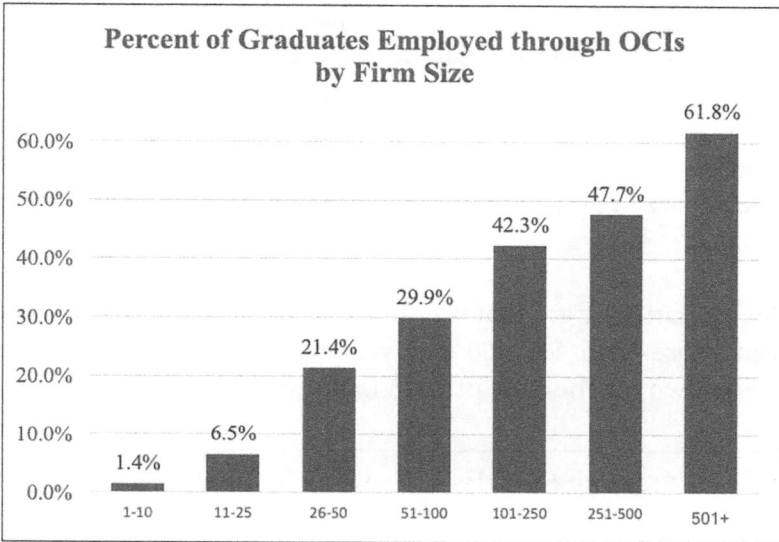

Chart 4 – NALP Class of 2018

The importance of OCIs is a function of the size of the law firm. Very few graduates find a job in the smallest firms through OCIs compared to the majority of students in the biggest firms. Graduates find jobs at small firms large through people they already know with 24.1% through self-initiated contacts or networking and 24.8% through referrals. CSO job listings represent another 22.5% of small firm jobs.[117]

Law Firm Salaries

Starting Salaries in Small Firms
Law students may look at the starting salaries of the smaller law firms compared to the larger law firms and not necessarily like what they see. For the class of 2018, all graduates going to law firm jobs had a median salary of $120,000 with firms of 1-10 lawyers showing a median of $60,000.[118] These numbers have a reporting bias because large firms report starting salaries more

frequently than smaller firms. Adjusting for these reporting biases, the true median salary for new graduates in law firms is $80,000 to $90,000 with an average of around $112,000.[119] Overall, small firms are more competitive in general and certainly worth considering when factoring in the number of hours worked and the non-monetary benefits of a small firm practice.

The majority of graduates entering a firm with 1-10 lawyers earn more than $50,000 per year as a starting salary. The breakdown for the class of 2018 looks like this:

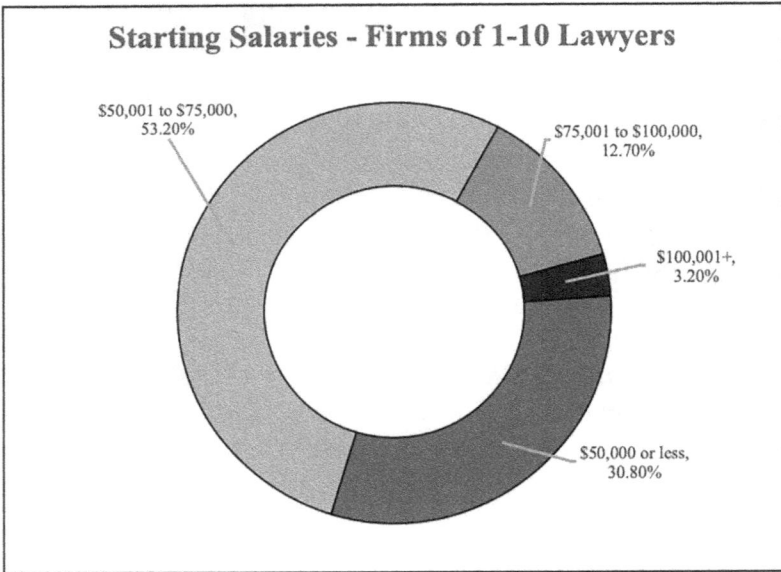

Starting Salaries - Firms of 1-10 Lawyers

$50,001 to $75,000, 53.20%

$75,001 to $100,000, 12.70%

$100,001+, 3.20%

$50,000 or less, 30.80%

Chart 5 – NALP Class of 2018[120]

In general, firms below 100 lawyers tend to average under $100,000 for starting salaries and firms with 101+ lawyers are above that threshold.[121] Small firms of 1-10 lawyers saw an average of $2,000 increase in starting salary from 2017 to 2018 while firms with 101+ lawyers stayed flat.[122]

Martindale-Avvo Attorney Compensation Report

Small Firm Salaries for All Practitioners
In a 2018 survey of almost 7,000 full time attorneys in solo and small law firms the average income was $194,000 with a median income of $135,000.[123] From 2017 to 2018, 49% of attorneys saw an increase in income while 31% stayed flat. For attorneys under age 35, a total of 86% saw an increase in income from 2017 to 2018.[124] Only 17% of full time attorneys reported supplemental income from non-legal services.[125]

Certain areas of practice earn more in solo and small practice than others. The top five practice areas for annual income are:
- Medical Malpractice: $267,000
- Personal Injury: $254,000
- Workers Compensation: $226,000
- Intellectual Property: $224,000
- Business: $218,000

The lower end of the scale includes immigration ($134,000), Probate ($137,000), and Bankruptcy ($140,000).[126]

There are some other differences in income as well. Small firm attorneys average $213,000 per year compared to $159,000 per year for solo attorney.[127] Additionally, in solo and small practice female attorneys earn on average 36% less than male attorney with $139,000 compared to $218,000 per year.[128]

Statistics Other Than Compensation
About three-quarters of attorneys (77%) in solo and small practice spend less than 20 hours per week meeting with clients or representing them in court, and just as many (76%) spend more than 20 hours working on billable work that does not involve meeting clients or going to court.[129] For non-billable work, 70% of attorneys spend less than 10 hours a week on it,

22% spend from 10 to 19 hours a week, and 5% spend 20 or more hours on non-billable work.[130]

Solo and small firms do not all have benefits that are offered to the attorneys. Benefits for attorneys:

- 25% of attorneys received no benefits
- 90% of employee attorneys received benefits
- 56% of solo attorneys have no benefits

Less than half of all attorneys have paid time off work, dental and vision insurance, and a retirement plan with an employer matching contribution.[131]

Attorneys reported the biggest difficulties they face in solo and small practice as follows:

- Difficult clients - 23%
- Business development - 17%
- Long Hours Worked - 17%

Sources

[1] Yale Law School Career Development Office, *The Truth About the Billable Hour* (2018), https://law.yale.edu/sites/default/files/area/department/cdo/document/billable_hour.pdf.

[2] The American Lawyer (Online), *Associates Just Want the Truth About Billable Hour Requirements* (July 30, 2019), Lexis Advance ("the most efficient attorneys bill only 75% or 80% of their time").

[3] National Association for Law Placement (NALP), *Update on Associate Hours Worked* (2016), https://www.nalp.org/0516research.

[4] The American Lawyer (Online), *Associates Just Want the Truth About Billable Hour Requirements* (July 30, 2019), Lexis Advance.

[5] The American Lawyer (Online), *Associates Just Want the Truth About Billable Hour Requirements* (July 30, 2019), Lexis Advance.

[6] Reddit, *What Is the Average Billable Hours Requirement For a Mid-sized Firm?*, https://www.reddit.com/r/LawSchool/comments/4whasy/what_is_the_average_billable_hours_requirement/.

[7] National Center for Education Statistics, Trends in Student Loan Debt for Graduate School Completers (2018), https://nces.ed.gov/programs/coe/indicator_tub.asp.

[8] Martindale-Avvo, *Attorney Compensation Report* 1 (2019).

[9] Alexander Y. Benikov, *How to Start a Law Practice* 32 (2017).

[10] Alexander Y. Benikov, *How to Start a Law Practice* 32 (2017).

[11] Note: Think about the hard work Kim Wexler put in calling potential clients in Season 2 of *Better Call Saul* only to see the firm, HHM, initially take Mesa Verde as a new client and leave Kim in document review as an ongoing punishment, large law firm style.

[12] Jay G. Foonberg, *How to Start & Build a Law Practice* 6-8 (1984).

[13] Jay G. Foonberg, *How to Start & Build a Law Practice* 5 (1984).

[14] Jay G. Foonberg, *How to Start & Build a Law Practice* 23 (1984).

[15] Jay G. Foonberg, *How to Start & Build a Law Practice* 23 (1984).

[16] The Lawyerist, *Guide to Starting a Law Firm* (Mar 20, 2020), https://lawyerist.com/starting-law-firm/.

[17] Gary Bauer, *Six Characteristics of Successful Solos – Work Ethic*, Solo Lawyer by Design (Jun 25, 2019), http://sololawyerbydesign.com/six-characteristics-of-successful-solos-work-ethic.

[18] The Lawyerist, *Guide to Starting a Law Firm* (Mar 20, 2020), https://lawyerist.com/starting-law-firm/.

[19] Alexander Y. Benikov, *How to Start a Law Practice* 27 (2017).

[20] The Lawyerist, *Guide to Starting a Law Firm* (Mar 20, 2020), https://lawyerist.com/starting-law-firm/.

[21] The Lawyerist, *Guide to Starting a Law Firm* (Mar 20, 2020), https://lawyerist.com/finance/insurance/.

[22] The Lawyerist, *Guide to Starting a Law Firm* (Mar 20, 2020), https://lawyerist.com/finance/insurance/.

[23] The Lawyerist, *Guide to Starting a Law Firm* (Mar 20, 2020), https://lawyerist.com/starting-law-firm/.

[24] Jay G. Foonberg, *How to Start & Build a Law Practice* 32-33 (1984).

[25] Jay G. Foonberg, *How to Start & Build a Law Practice* 33 (1984).

[26] Gary Bauer, *Financing Your Practice—Shared Office Space*, Law Practice Today (Apr 14, 2020), https://www.lawpracticetoday.org/article/financing-practice-shared-office-space/.

[27] Jay G. Foonberg, *How to Start & Build a Law Practice* 34 (1984).

[28] Gary Bauer, *Financing Your Practice—Shared Office Space*, Law Practice Today (Apr 14, 2020),

[29] The Lawyerist, *Remote Work & Virtual Law Firms* (Apr 22, 2020), https://lawyerist.com/technology/virtual-law-firm/.

[30] Marcia Watson Wasserman, *Virtual Is the New Law Firm Reality*, American Bar Association (May 1, 2019), https://www.americanbar.org/groups/law_practice/publications/law_practice_magazine/2019/MJ2019/MJ19Wasserman/.

[31] The Lawyerist, *New Law Firm Basic Technology Shopping List* (Nov 12, 2019), https://lawyerist.com/blog/solo-technology-shopping-list-basics/.

[32] Ryan Harnedy, *What is 3-2-1 backup?*, Carbonite (Jan 29, 2016), https://www.carbonite.com/blog/article/2016/01/what-is-3-2-1-backup.

[33] Michael Muchmore and Ben Moore, *The Best Online Backup Services for 2020*, PC Magazine (Dec 24, 2019), https://www.pcmag.com/picks/the-best-online-backup-services.

[34] Michael Muchmore and Ben Moore, *The Best Online Backup Services for 2020*, PC Magazine (Dec 24, 2019), https://www.pcmag.com/picks/the-best-online-backup-services.

[35] The Lawyerist, *New Law Firm Basic Technology Shopping List* (Nov 12, 2019), https://lawyerist.com/blog/solo-technology-shopping-list-basics/.

[36] Alexander Y. Benikov, *How to Start a Law Practice* 118 (2017).

[37] Randall Ryder, *How to Get Clients as a New Lawyer*, The Lawyerist (Jan 22, 2020), https://lawyerist.com/blog/how-to-get-your-first-client/.

[38] Randall Ryder, *How to Get Clients as a New Lawyer*, The Lawyerist (Jan 22, 2020), https://lawyerist.com/blog/how-to-get-your-first-client/.

[39] Randall Ryder, *How to Get Clients as a New Lawyer*, The Lawyerist (Jan 22, 2020), https://lawyerist.com/blog/how-to-get-your-first-client/.

[40] Jay G. Foonberg, *How to Start & Build a Law Practice* 85 (1984).

[41] Stephan Futeral, *Managing Your Law Firm's Online Reputation*, JustLegal (Feb 5, 2016), https://www.justlegalmarketing.com/online-reviews-lawyers/.

[42] The Lawyerist, *Law Firm Client Reviews & Reputation Management* (Mar 23, 2020), https://lawyerist.com/marketing/client-reviews-reputation/.

[43] Gerald G. Goldberg, *Practical Lawyering* 116 (2009).

[44] Jay G. Foonberg, *How to Start & Build a Law Practice* 93 (1984).

[45] Jay G. Foonberg, *How to Start & Build a Law Practice* 93 (1984).

[46] Jay G. Foonberg, *How to Start & Build a Law Practice* 63 (1984).

[47] Alexander Y. Benikov, *How to Start a Law Practice* 17 (2017).

[48] Alexander Y. Benikov, *How to Start a Law Practice* 16-17 (2017).

[49] Alexander Y. Benikov, *How to Start a Law Practice* 69 (2017).

[50] Alexander Y. Benikov, *How to Start a Law Practice* 69 (2017).

[51] The Lawyerist, *Complete Guide to the Best Law Firm Websites* (Apr 24, 2020), https://lawyerist.com/marketing/websites/.

[52] Mark Homer, *FAQ: Do I Really Need A Law Firm Blog?*, GNGF (June 18, 2018), https://gngf.com/faq-do-i-really-need-a-law-firm-blog/.

[53] *Bates v. State Bar of Arizona*, 433 U.S. 350 (1977).

[54] Model Rules of Professional Conduct, Rule 7.2(b).

[55] Elizabeth Stawicki, *Lawyer advertising still controversial after 30 years*, MPR News (July 9, 2007), https://www.mprnews.org/story/2007/07/09/lawyer-advertising-still-controversial-after-30-years.

[56] Elizabeth Stawicki, *Lawyer advertising still controversial after 30 years*, MPR News (July 9, 2007), https://www.mprnews.org/story/2007/07/09/lawyer-advertising-still-controversial-after-30-years.

[57] Elizabeth Stawicki, *Lawyer advertising still controversial after 30 years*, MPR News (July 9, 2007), https://www.mprnews.org/story/2007/07/09/lawyer-advertising-still-controversial-after-30-years.

[58] Alexander Y. Benikov, *How to Start a Law Practice* 67 (2017).

[59] Alexander Y. Benikov, *How to Start a Law Practice* 106 (2017).

[60] Alexander Y. Benikov, *How to Start a Law Practice* 106 (2017).

[61] Alexander Y. Benikov, *How to Start a Law Practice* 133 (2017).

[62] Jay G. Foonberg, *How to Start & Build a Law Practice* 24 (1984).

[63] Gerald G. Goldberg, *Practical Lawyering* 103 (2009).

[64] Jay G. Foonberg, *How to Start & Build a Law Practice* 55 (1984).

[65] Gerald G. Goldberg, *Practical Lawyering* 9 (2009).

[66] Martindale-Avvo, *Attorney Compensation Report* 12 (2019).

[67] Alexander Y. Benikov, *How to Start a Law Practice* 88 (2017).

[68] Jay G. Foonberg, *How to Start & Build a Law Practice* 128 (1984).

[69] Alexander Y. Benikov, *How to Start a Law Practice* 86 (2017).

[70] Jay G. Foonberg, *How to Start & Build a Law Practice* 144 (1984).

[71] Jay G. Foonberg, *How to Start & Build a Law Practice* 119 (1984).

[72] Jay G. Foonberg, *How to Start & Build a Law Practice* 121 (1984).

[73] Jay G. Foonberg, *How to Start & Build a Law Practice* 121 (1984).

[74] Alexander Y. Benikov, *How to Start a Law Practice* 87 (2017).

[75] Teresa Matich, *A Guide to Evergreen Retainers for Law Firms*, Clio (June 13, 2018), https://www.clio.com/blog/evergreen-retainers-law-firms/.

[76] Ryan Mayer, *Why would I pay for a consultation when I can get a "Free Consultation"*, Kelly Thompson Family Law (May 2, 2016), http://kellythompsonfamilylaw.com/2016/05/02/why-would-i-pay-for-a-consultation-when-i-can-get-a-free-consultation/.

[77] Ryan Mayer, *Why would I pay for a consultation when I can get a "Free Consultation"*, Kelly Thompson Family Law (May 2, 2016), http://kellythompsonfamilylaw.com/2016/05/02/why-would-i-pay-for-a-consultation-when-i-can-get-a-free-consultation/.

[78] Model Rules of Professional Conduct, Rule 5.4(b).

[79] Model Rules of Professional Conduct, Rule 1.16, Comment 1.

[80] Randall Ryder, *Bad Clients You Don't Take Will Be the Best Money You Never Made*, The Lawyerist (Mar 24, 2017), https://lawyerist.com/blog/bad-clients/.

[81] Gerald G. Goldberg, *Practical Lawyering* 15 (2009).

[82] Randall Ryder, *Bad Clients You Don't Take Will Be the Best Money You Never Made*, The Lawyerist (Mar 24, 2017), https://lawyerist.com/blog/bad-clients/.

[83] Jay G. Foonberg, *How to Start & Build a Law Practice* 96 (1984).

[84] Alexander Y. Benikov, *How to Start a Law Practice* 93 (2017).

[85] Randall Ryder, *Bad Clients You Don't Take Will Be the Best Money You Never Made*, The Lawyerist (Mar 24, 2017), https://lawyerist.com/blog/bad-clients/.

[86] Jay G. Foonberg, *How to Start & Build a Law Practice* 100-01 (1984).

[87] Alexander Y. Benikov, *How to Start a Law Practice* 39 (2017).

[88] Model Rules of Professional Conduct, Rule 1.16, Comment 4.

[89] Model Rules of Professional Conduct, Rule 1.16(b)(1).

[90] Model Rules of Professional Conduct, Rule 1.16(b).

[91] Model Rules of Professional Conduct, Rule 1.16(d).

[92] Model Rules of Professional Conduct, Rule 1.16(d).

[93] Professor Donald Gjerdingen, Lecture, Maurer School of Law, Spring 2019.

[94] Dina Roth Port, Lawyers weigh in: Why is there a depression epidemic in the profession?, ABA Journal (May 11, 2018), https://www.abajournal.com/voice/article/lawyers_weigh_in_why_is_there_a_depression_epidemic_in_the_profession.

[95] Dina Roth Port, Lawyers weigh in: Why is there a depression epidemic in the profession?, ABA Journal (May 11, 2018), https://www.abajournal.com/voice/article/lawyers_weigh_in_why_is_there_a_depression_epidemic_in_the_profession.

[96] Alexander Y. Benikov, *How to Start a Law Practice* 14 (2017).

[97] Wendy Werner, *Five Ways to Find a Mentor*, Attorney at Work (July 27, 2012), https://www.attorneyatwork.com/five-ways-to-find-a-mentor/.

[98] Wendy Werner, *Five Ways to Find a Mentor*, Attorney at Work (July 27, 2012), https://www.attorneyatwork.com/five-ways-to-find-a-mentor/.

[99] Wendy Werner, *Five Ways to Find a Mentor*, Attorney at Work (July 27, 2012), https://www.attorneyatwork.com/five-ways-to-find-a-mentor/.

[100] Alexander Y. Benikov, *How to Start a Law Practice* 18 (2017).

[101] Kerriann Stout, *How to Find and Keep the Perfect Mentor*, Above the Law (Nov 13, 2017), https://abovethelaw.com/2017/11/how-to-find-and-keep-the-perfect-mentor/.

[102] Randall Ryder, *How to Ask Another Attorney for Help*, The Lawyerist (Jan 15, 2020), https://lawyerist.com/blog/ask-another-attorney-help/.

[103] Randall Ryder, *How to Ask Another Attorney for Help*, The Lawyerist (Jan 15, 2020), https://lawyerist.com/blog/ask-another-attorney-help/.

[104] Randall Ryder, *How to Ask Another Attorney for Help*, The Lawyerist (Jan 15, 2020), https://lawyerist.com/blog/ask-another-attorney-help/.

[105] Alexander Y. Benikov, *How to Start a Law Practice* 15 (2017).

[106] Model Rules of Professional Conduct, Rule 1.3, Comment 3.

[107] Model Rules of Professional Conduct, Rule 1.17, Comment 11.

[108] Model Rules of Professional Conduct, Rule 1.17, Comment 1.

[109] Alexander Y. Benikov, *How to Start a Law Practice* 125 (2017).

[110] Alexander Y. Benikov, *How to Start a Law Practice* 125 (2017).

[111] Steven D. Price, *The World's Funniest Lawyer Jokes: A Caseload of Jurisprudential Jests* 114-18 (2011).

[112] Bureau of the Census, *North American Industry Classification System* 461 (2017), https://www.census.gov/eos/www/naics/2017NAICS/2017_NAICS_Manual.pdf.

[113] National Association for Law Placement (NALP), *Jobs & JDs: Employment and Salaries of New Law Graduates Class of 2018* 45 (2019).

[114] National Association for Law Placement (NALP), *Jobs & JDs: Employment and Salaries of New Law Graduates Class of 2018* 38 (2019).

[115] National Association for Law Placement (NALP), *Jobs & JDs: Employment and Salaries of New Law Graduates Class of 2018* 39 (2019).

[116] National Association for Law Placement (NALP), *Jobs & JDs: Employment and Salaries of New Law Graduates Class of 2018* 133 (2019).

[117] National Association for Law Placement (NALP), *Jobs & JDs: Employment and Salaries of New Law Graduates Class of 2018* 133 (2019).

[118] National Association for Law Placement (NALP), *Jobs & JDs: Employment and Salaries of New Law Graduates Class of 2018* 38 (2019).

[119] National Association for Law Placement (NALP), *Jobs & JDs: Employment and Salaries of New Law Graduates Class of 2018* 39 (2019).

[120] National Association for Law Placement (NALP), *Jobs & JDs: Employment and Salaries of New Law Graduates Class of 2018* 42 (2019).

[121] National Association for Law Placement (NALP), *Jobs & JDs: Employment and Salaries of New Law Graduates Class of 2018* 42 (2019).

[122] National Association for Law Placement (NALP), *Jobs & JDs: Employment and Salaries of New Law Graduates Class of 2018* 39 (2019).

[123] Martindale-Avvo, *Attorney Compensation Report* 1 (2019).

[124] Martindale-Avvo, *Attorney Compensation Report* 3 (2019).

[125] Martindale-Avvo, *Attorney Compensation Report* 4 (2019).

[126] Martindale-Avvo, *Attorney Compensation Report* 2 (2019).

[127] Martindale-Avvo, *Attorney Compensation Report* 8 (2019).

[128] Martindale-Avvo, *Attorney Compensation Report* 6 (2019).

[129] Martindale-Avvo, *Attorney Compensation Report* 13-14 (2019).

[130] Martindale-Avvo, *Attorney Compensation Report* 15 (2019).

[131] Martindale-Avvo, *Attorney Compensation Report* 9 (2019).